A HOUSE WITHOUT MEATBALLS

An Unforgettable Autobiography

Chapbook Press

Schuler Books
2660 28th Street SE
Grand Rapids, MI 49512
(616) 942-7330
www.schulerbooks.com

ISBN 13: 9781943359752

Library of Congress Control Number: 2017949309

Copyright © 2017 Vincent Herr
All rights reserved.

No part of this book may be reproduced in any form without express permission of the copyright holder.

Printed in the United States by Chapbook Press.

Dedicated to those whose lives are affected by

Dyslexia,

Children of divorce,

And those who seek to know their true origin.

Special thanks to my wife Peggy, for all the love and support

Thanks to Jim Henson; for the joy you gave to my children and me

Mr. Rogers for his kind and gentle nature, and it's you I like Mr. Rogers

The Four Freshman, for not only their beautiful harmony, but also their wonderful lyrics

To The Dave Brubeck Quartet, whose rhythms and sounds run through my mind everyday

The sweet sound of Paul Desmond

Frank Sinatra, you're beautiful

And to all those other artists that have given me great joy

Thank you NPR and PBS for the news you delivered to me over the years

Al Roker for your determination and wit

Lester Holt for your suave broadcasts

Charlie Rose for your brilliant, in depth interviews

Thank you Robin Williams, for all the brilliant work you've done

And to the movie What Dreams May Come

Hugh Hefner thank you for all the opportunities you gave musicians to work on your stage, including me

WARNING!

This book contains name dropping in order to emphasize my point that even though I live with a learning disability, and Dyslexia, I still worked with many creative people in my time. It was an honor, and I want all those who may be affected by a learning disability to know that there are no limitations to what you can do.

TABLE OF CONTENTS

CHAPTER 1.....THE BEGINNING

CHAPTER 2.....KITTY AND THE ALY KATS

CHAPTER 3.....THE BREAKFAST COUNTER

CHAPTER 4.....YOUR FATHER'S MUSTACHE

CHAPTER 5.....THE MAILBOX

CHAPTER 6.....IT HAPPENED ONE NIGHT

CHAPTER 7.....THE DAY I MET A WAITRESS

CHAPTER 8.....SHE WAS SPEAKING GREEK

CHAPTER 9.....TERROR IN THE NIGHT

CHAPTER 10.....THE TRIAL

CHAPTER 11.....THE RELEASE

CHAPTER 12.....AT LAST

CHAPTER 13.....THE FIRE

CHAPTER 14.....ALWAYS AND FOREVER

CHAPTER 15.....THE TRUTH COMES OUT

THE BEGINNING

It's been said that you are what you are before you're even born. Your mother and father, even before they met, had you inside of them. Their genes, culture, and emotions all have an influence on who you will be, even though you, ultimately, will have your own personality.

This is a true story about my childhood and my life experiences, as well as a search for what I now know as my true DNA. As you read, you will realize that I was raised in a dysfunctional family. I was lonely, confused, insecure and in near-constant turmoil. I was one of the first latch key kids to come home to an empty house. I also struggled with dyslexia, also called word blindness, along with what is now known as ADHD, a disability which made it hard for me to read, spell, memorize, or learn. But I have found that I am part of a group of thousands of successful and creative people that live with this learning disability. Richard Branson, Steven Spielberg, Jay Leno, Steve Jobs, Henry Winkler, and Pablo Picasso, to name a few, all suffer from dyslexia. Personally I call it the creative curse. I can't shut it off! I'm always thinking of ideas and inventions, 24 hours a day, 7 days a week. It's a left brain right brain condition.

On June 9, 1942, 3 years before I was born, Hitler's army marched into the little city of Lidice, Czechoslovakia, which at the time had a population of 300. On June 10 at 7 am the Nazis, on Hitler's orders, shot 173 men and boys, as well as some women. The remaining women were sent to a concentration camp, where they were later killed. The Nazis then burned the city to the ground. The world was horrified at this atrocity. These were innocent people. War is war, but this brutality was inhumane.

      One day a developer, Dominic A Romano, who was from Joliet, Illinois, near Chicago, received a phone call from Washington D.C. The call was from Winston Churchill, and President Roosevelt. They asked if he would rename his subdivision, which was under construction, in memory of the tragedy that happened in Lidice. Mr. Romano agreed to rename the subdivision Lidice, and went on to build 300 homes and a monument with a rose garden in memory of the people of Czechoslovakia. He was the first person in the world to rename an extinguished town. 82 rose bushes were planted in memory, of the 82 children murdered in Chelmno; an extermination camp where the children were brought to, and executed.

      There was an emotional ceremony held, once the subdivision was complete. In attendance was the exiled President of Czechoslovakia, the Governor of Illinois, Otto Koerner, Marshall Fields the department store owner, along with many other celebrated people. In addition, a live radio broadcast which went overseas, happened to be the first broadcast of its time to be heard behind the Iron Curtain. At this event a powerful speech was delivered by Mr. Romano, "Lest We Forget", which echoed the tragedies of Hitler's brutality throughout WWII.

This is my story, and I'm sticking to it!

I was born October 25, 1945 at 3:36 a.m. Length 19', weight 5 lbs 10 oz. Wow, I was a big guy! That year the hit song was Perry Como's "Till the end of time". In baseball, the World Series was being played between the Detroit Tigers and Chicago Cubs. The Tigers won.

I was brought from the hospital, to a new small home in the subdivision named Lidice, built by Mr. Romano. I had met Mr. Romano on many occasions, for many different reasons. He was short, with thick black hair, and wire rimmed glasses. He always wore a pin striped suit with cuff links, a tie, and a fedora hat. His car was a big Cadillac. Dominic always seemed to show up at the strangest times and places. I felt like he would always be parked on various corners, waiting for us. I was always with my mother in the car when she would stop to talk to him. He would stand on the driver's side and talk to her through the open window. I remember mother always made me kiss him on the cheek every time. She would always tell me to kiss Mr. Romano. I thought to myself, why? I remember he would walk around the front of the car over to the passenger side where I was, take off his fedora hat, lean in the window, and I would kiss him on the cheek. I remember he had very dark skin. Then she would always repeat "Don't tell your dad you saw Mr. Romano." Why was this a secret?

The subdivision where I lived, also had a strip mall. It housed a gas station, grocery store, drugstore with a soda fountain, root beer stand, hardware store, and best of all the movie theater. The bus on the city route was named Lidice, of which I took often in my younger years. This is where I lived until the age of 13.

Now on with my story.

From my earliest memories I knew something was wrong. It would appear to someone else, that everything was perfectly normal. But I knew something was very disturbing. Why was it disturbing you may ask? There are just some things inside the mind and body that just don't feel right. It's like I was switched at birth. I felt like I'd been sent home to the wrong family. Some of my earliest childhood memories are that my parents never talked. They yelled. They were always yelling, every day. Mom would come home from work and start it.

"Glenn, were you drinking?" she would ask.

Dad did drink every day. Shots, and beer, but he was a good drunk not mean. Then the arguing would start, and it would go on for hours and hours.

Dad was a passive man. Born and raised on a farm, he learned to plant seeds, and be patient to watch the fruits and vegetables grow at a young age. He had two brothers, and two sisters. They all worked the farm in their younger days with their parents.

He was also very gentle with animals, small and large. He would tell stories about when he chose to sleep in the barn all night, to wait for the birth of a foal. I believe he even had a pet pig. He would also hang around the kitchen with his mother, where he learned to cook a lot of German food.
There were no meatballs. I remember it was a wood stove that his mother had, very old and traditional, where he first learned to cook. When he married my mother and moved away from the farm, I truly believe he became a very lonely man, for the rest of his life. The loss of that lifestyle was a huge contributor to his loneliness.

When he left the farm, he moved to the town of Joliet, where he worked as a furnace repair man. He was also a volunteer fireman for the subdivision where we lived. Mr. Romano had built the fire station in 1942, and it housed two fire trucks. After work, Dad would pick me up from home, and say "Gotta go to the store to get dinner." Before we got to the store he always made a stop at the bar for a few minutes, or longer. He would drink beer out of the bottle, and shots from little paper cups. I remember being there with him and jumping around on all the beer cases that were piled up in the back room of the bar, while he would drink. After that, we would go to the store, or go home so he could cook dinner for me.

He was also the one who took me to doctor

appointments. Man that was scary. You see the doctor looked like Boris Karloff from the movies. Remember Frankenstein? This guy had a big head and he smoked. He would sit down, look at me, and blow smoke right in my face. I understand he was the doctor that also delivered me.

I remember once I was playing around with the neighbor kids, and fell and cut my forehead. It was a Saturday, and Mom was working at the beauty shop. I was bleeding, so Dad took me to Dr. Muncie's office. I was sitting in the waiting room with a few other little boys, holding a washcloth on my head to stop up the little bit of bleeding. There was a boy next to me who was reading a comic book; he was with his dad also. I thought to myself, "Why is he here?" and, "I bet they call me first because I'm bleeding." Well, they called him first and as he walked by me he was still holding the comic book like nothing was wrong, but stuck on the back of his head was this big fish lure. It was dangling as he walked by, flapping around like it was still baiting a large mouth bass. Now I knew why they called him first. Apparently he and his dad were out fishing, and when his dad went to cast his line he stuck his son in the back of the head with the lure. These are the kinds of stories from your childhood that you just don't forget.

Dad liked being in the kitchen. He loved to cook. I remember he always had these big cast-iron skillets sizzling away on the stove-top. He would use these big old pots to cook things like vegetable soup. His vegetable soup was the best; it was homey, all-American, comfort food. He also had a good garden planted in the backyard. Although it was nothing like the 600 acre farm that he had grown up on, he took such pride in it. There were rows of tomato plants, peppers, onions, and I believe, eggplant. I can picture him now, going out to tend his garden. Carrying a bucket, pulling the weeds, and watering the plants.

But every moment, there in the same house, was filled with the constant bickering between mom and dad. I was always scared, and disappointed. I would hide in my room, and put the radio on so I couldn't hear them. It went on for hours and hours, a constant stressor in my childhood life.

I always knew something was wrong when I looked at my parents. They did not look like my parents, and I suppose that's pretty funny in itself. What are your parents supposed to look like? My mother certainly, without a doubt was my mother. My dad, however, was of German descent, and Pennsylvania Dutch. Man, did you ever see those guys? They're like the Amish with the big hats, beards, pitch forks, and they always traveled by horse and buggy.

As I mentioned earlier, dad came from a farm in the middle of Illinois. It was known as the Herr farm. His siblings were all farmers as well, and they farmed 600 acres that his parents owned.

I was very young when I first visited the Herr Farm, so I

don't remember much. I do remember it was a big old farmhouse seated of the highway near El Paso, Illinois. It contained a gigantic winding staircase that led to an oval shaped second floor, where the bedrooms were located. I remember the bathroom contained a pedestal sink, which I'd never seen before. As well, the house also had a back stair case that led into the kitchen. There were also several big barns on the property. I can recall playing with my cousins on the hay stacks up in some of the barns.

  Dad told me stories about farming as a child. Clydesdale horses would pull their plows. These were big horses, like those that currently pull the Budweiser wagon. They would plow and plant all day long, and that was all he knew. There was no electricity when he was a child, nor automobiles. The farm was a few miles outside of a small town called El Paso, Illinois, about 130 miles south of Chicago. The Rev. Bishop Sheen, who would go on to be famous on both radio and television, was one of their neighbors. Rumor has it, Rev. Bishop Sheen ice skated with my dad and his siblings, on a frozen lake in the back 40.

  Dad's youngest brother, Duane, was in the Air Force in World War II. He was a belly gunner in a Bell P-52. It was shot down over Germany, and the crew had to parachute out. They were captured by the Germans, and forced to walk naked through the streets before being put into a concentration camp. He was imprisoned in the camp hospital for a period of time, because he had been shot through the leg, and I believe another part of his body. Once he was well enough, he lived out the rest of his time in the concentration camp, until the war was over. When he was released, he came to visit us in Joliet on his way back to the farm. He told us many stories of Germans, and the concentration camp hospital. He said that while he was in the hospital, they favored him because his last name was Herr, which translates to Mr. or gentlemen in German. Apparently they weren't so nice to the other American soldiers who lay in beds next to him. There were stories he told us, of the soldiers slapping other patients across the face, for no reason at all.

    He once told a story to us of a German officer, who came up to him and said, "We know where you live, we know your neighbors, we know your brothers and sisters, and your parents' names." He then recited their names, and they were correct. "We also have information that your brother and sister-in-law just gave birth to a baby boy." That baby was me. I don't know how the Germans had such knowledge in those days, without computers and social media. But they did. It's terribly frightening to think about.

    My mother was from a small town in Illinois called Minonk, about 11 miles from El Paso. She had red hair and blue eyes that always appeared to be glowing. She was one of five sisters, whom she remained close to for her entire life. She and dad met at a dance, or a social activity many years ago. They got married and moved to Joliet, about a hundred miles from Dad's farm. Joliet was no Chicago, but to them it was the biggest city they'd ever lived in.

I have a brother Sam, who is eleven years older than me. How the story goes is that he was born at the farmhouse in El Paso, on a visit one weekend during a heavy storm, with rain, lightning, and thunder. That was 1934. It may sound funny to you, but I thought there was something wrong about him. I did not feel he was my brother. You see I have very dark skin and very black hair, while he is much taller and has lighter hair. Sam resembles the Herr family, of German decent. I stick out like I sore thumb! I appear to be of more Mediterranean descent.

I can only, maybe, remember one single meal my mother ever cooked. She never cooked for us, since she worked, and was rarely ever home. She had a small beauty shop business, would leave the house very early, and not come home until very late. I do remember, however, Mom would make me Jell-O with fruit cocktail in it just before she would leave for work. I think she thought that was healthy, but we all now know it was really just all sugar. Mom had very bad asthma all through my childhood, and she always had a hard time breathing. Sometimes, just walking from the car to the house, she would have to sit down and use her inhaler.

I don't remember my older brother being around the house much, because he was eleven years older than me and already grown up. But dad was always there to care for me. He always cooked food special for me. I have very early memories of sitting in a high chair, as a young child, in the kitchen. The funny thing is, I knew that somehow the food was wrong. Even though Dad was a very good cook, it never felt like the food I was supposed to eat. I mean, what's with this sauerkraut? How would a child so young know that the food was not ethnically right? Isn't it strange? It seems in our heart and soul, we know our ethnic background. Food likes, and dislikes... You can feel when something is wrong. It's almost like having a pain in your appendix. You go to the doctor, he removes the appendix, and then your pain is gone. I knew inside of me that something was wrong, but I had no doctor to remedy my situation. I could feel this from my earliest memories starting at around one year of age. As it turns out, I could feel it for the rest of my life! Every day of the week, still, I have this disturbing disconnection with my family. Including aunts, uncles, and all kinds of distant relatives! The kids I played with down the block were all strange looking, just like I thought my aunts and uncles were. There was this one kid they called bulldog, and he looked like a bulldog. I saw about as much resemblance between my aunts, and uncles, and I, as I saw between me, and him.

    There was a lady who lived across the street. She was, for lack of a better word, nuts. She would stand in her front yard with a mirror held up, flashing at the sun, calling everybody in the neighborhood names. She was eventually taken away, and put into a sanitarium. When you're a kid and you hear that word, that's scary. Our parents would threaten us with "If you're not good we will to send you away to the sanitarium" so we behaved. I also remember this older man, who would walk down the street screaming "Sharpen knives! Sharpen knives!" He would carry his big grinding stone on his back. It was heavy, so he was always bent over. Then the wives would come out of their houses with their knives to be sharpened. My mother was not one of them, for she was always working at her beauty shop, which coincidentally was just around the corner from Mr. Romano's office. I was the only kid on the block that did not have a mother at home to make lunch for me. Anyways, he would set up this little grinding stone on the side of the street and sharpen knives for whatever change he could get.

  We also had a crazy mailman on our street. We called him Mad Maddie. He was kind of a big guy, shell shocked from the war, and had a big scar going from his head down past his nose to his lip. He also had a steel plate in his head. Whenever the kids would see the mailman coming down the street, we'd all run and hide. One of the kids would always yell "Here comes Mad Maddie! He's got a steel plate in his head! He's shell shocked!"

  I remember there was one time we had a cereal box with a picture of a toy submarine that you could order, printed on it. I showed it to my friend Richie, and couple of the other boys on the block. It looked real neat. You could put baking soda in the boat, fill the bathtub with water, and watch it sink then resurface, or at least that's how it was advertised on the cereal box. There were about six of us little boys that ordered the submarine, and we would hide in the bushes waiting for it every day. One of the kids would yell out "Here comes Mad Maddie! He's got a steel plate in his head! He's shell shocked!" One day Mad Maddie was carrying some little boxes in his bag, and he delivered one to each of our doors. We waited in the bushes until he'd gone down the street then we all ran home. I anxiously opened up the box. There it was, my submarine. Except this one was about the size of a harmonica, and made from cheap plastic. It looked nothing like the picture!

  Regardless, I ran into the bathroom, filled the tub up with water, and put the baking soda in the bottom of the submarine, just like the instruction had told me. Then I watched it sink. It did eventually rise to the surface, but it was belly up. After all this time, and all this excitement, it was the dullest toy I'd ever had. I guess that was my first lesson in advertising. This thing was so small it almost went down the drain! I figured I would go back to my toy train. It was a Lionel, which was the best!

  One day I was riding my bike, and I fell on the gravel in the middle of the street. The bike was laying on top of me, and I couldn't get it off! All of a sudden I looked up, and there's Mad Maddie looking down at me! That big head, and that scar coming down from his head to his lip. I could just hear the kids yelling out "Its mad Maddie! He's got a steel plate in his head! He's shell shocked! Run! Run!" I was so scared. He lifted the bike off of me with one hand, picked me up with the other, brushed me off a little, and walked me home while carrying, not only his big mail bag, but my bike, and still holding my hand. He was like the Incredible Hulk. I suppose that was the day I learned a very good lesson: You should not judge people by rumors. I knew then that he was a very caring gentle man, who helped me when I most needed it. I never did know his real name. I suppose it was Maddie, but from that day on I stopped joining in on the name calling.

I just called him Maddie.

There was this one family of thirteen kids that lived down the street. They were a strong German Catholic family, and one of their boys became my childhood playmate. Their house also smelled like sauerkraut, and I didn't know how anybody could eat that stuff. One time I had lunch at their house, and it was the first time I ever saw a gallon of milk. There were two of these heavy glass gallon bottles of milk sitting on the table. I went home and I said to Dad, "Could you buy a gallon of milk?" He told me it would take two weeks to drink a gallon of milk, since it was just my older brother and I. I said to him "Richie's family drinks two full gallons every meal." He simply laughed and replied "Well they've got thirteen kids!"

One time I went down to Richie's house about seven o'clock at night. I knocked on the door and no one answered, so I looked in the window. It was weird. They were all sitting around the living room in chairs in a circle. I know they heard me at the door, so why didn't they answer? I thought it was the weirdest thing. In those days there was a lot of talk about Martians coming down to earth, and blending in with ordinary families. I thought maybe Richie's family might secretly be space Martians in disguise. I didn't know what was going on, so I ran home, locked myself in my bedroom, put on my uncle's army helmet, grabbed my flashlight, and hid under the covers. But the Martians never came. I later found out they were saying the Rosary because they were Catholic. That was my first experience with the Catholic religion. My parents always sent me to the Presbyterian Church, where I would hide out with a few other boys in the basement, until the service was over. Actually, it was disappointing the Richie's family weren't Martians. Because if they were, they could've taken me to space to play with some new friends. After all they couldn't be any weirder looking than the kids on the block. Maybe there were meatballs in their spaceship, get rid of the sauerkraut!

Richie's brothers had a paper route. Yes, in those days we had paper routes! It was handed down to Richie. I believe it was 100 papers he needed to deliver, seven days a week. He asked me to be his helper. So there I was, about nine years old, at my first job as a paperboy. The route was about five blocks, on both sides. Richie would take one street for five blocks, and I would take the next Street for five blocks, so we could cover both sides of the street. We passed out papers every day, rain or shine, in the cold and snow. Dad would always get me dressed for the cold. He bought me these engineer boots, and always buttoned my coat so that I was warm. I then would go down to Richie's to get the papers. Soon I would have my second hint of being dyslexic.

Did I mentioned that this book is about being dyslexic? And having a learning disorder? The first time I knew I had problems, was when my mother sent me to dance school for tap and ballet. I could never remember the steps no matter how hard I tried. We had this big dance recital once at the beautiful Rialto Theater. I had a snazzy costume, and I looked good! But I was always out of step because I just could not learn the moves.

Back to my paper route.

We would have to count the papers, put them in our bag, and make sure that some of the grumpy old men on the route got special attention. There was a special way we had to fold these papers, and it depended on how many pages for the day. Usually, Sunday papers were the biggest by far. On Sundays, we could only do half the route. We would fold the majority of the papers at Richie's house, put them in our bag, and then head out to deliver as many as we could carry. But we always had to go back for the rest. On days when there were just a few pages, we would fold the papers one way, it was a bit like a triangle, and Richie could throw it like a Frisbee right at the door.

I could not learn to fold paper the way Richie, and all of his brothers before him did. I would try, and try, and try, and when I could not get it, I made up my own way. It wasn't as good as Richie's, but I got the paper to the door most of the time. Almost every day, when I would walk up to the door with the paper, customers would say "What's the headlines today, kid?" I couldn't read the headline so I didn't know. I would always say "oh just the same old thing." One man asked me "What's the headlines today, kid?" and I replied to him "Oh I don't know, Hitler bombed another city in Europe." He stared at me in the strangest way and said "The war's been over for 10 years!" I told him I was just kidding. I didn't tell him I couldn't read the headlines.

Remember in the old movies a paperboy would stand on a corner yelling, "Read all about it, read all about it"? I remembered that. So from that day forward whenever someone would ask "What's in the headlines today Kid?" I would yell "Read all about it, you can read all about it!"

In the winter, Richie and I had a pocket warmer. It was like a big cigarette lighter that you actually lit and put in your pocket. It had some type of wick that glowed, and then you could put the top on and carry in your pocket. It didn't catch fire, it only kept you warm. I remember mine was red and I believe Richie's was silver. I don't know if they still make them or not, but I heard some kids caught their pants on fire.

I was paid $2.50 a week. By the end of the year, I'd actually saved enough money to buy a Daisy BB gun. Richie also got one, and we used to shoot at cans on a fence post together. We'd shoot at them just in like the Western movies we would watch, pretending we were outlaws and desperadoes. We shot at other things too, but I won't talk about that. The statute of limitations might still be in effect. After all, it was just a couple of streetlights, and maybe a couple of small windows on an old garage, and, oh no, I'm not going to tell all. We were just kids. Remember the movie *A Christmas Story*? When Ralphie gets a BB gun, his dad says "Careful kid, you'll shoot your eye out." That's because when you shoot a BB gun it can ricochet and come back and hit you. One time Richie shot himself right in the foot. It swelled up very big, and we had to cut his tennis shoe off. For the next week, he walked with a limp, including when he passed papers.

I was lonely, during those earlier days. Although we did have one of the first TVs in our neighborhood. I would watch cartoons and westerns: Gene Autry, cowboys fighting Indians. I was too young to realize how wrong that was at the time! I would also watch the movies about spaceships, and little green men coming to earth. My parents never read to me. I never knew what nursery rhymes were. I could not read the simplest book.

Believe me, I tried. Sally met Jane, or Dick and Harry, or something like that. I also could never read comic books. They were always so confusing to me. I know a lot of kids would sit down for hours at a time to read them, but I was too hyper, and I just could not concentrate. I always knew something was wrong.

I remember once my mother took me to the eye doctor to see if an eye condition was causing my reading problems. The eye doctor examined me. I read words, and letters from a board across the room. He just shook his head slowly back and forth several times, and then said to my mother "His eyes are fine."

I remember another time I was playing with the neighborhood kids, and we were sledding down a hill close to my house. I went home to warm up because I was cold, and my brother said to me, "Tie your shoes before you go back out." I think I was seven or eight, maybe younger, and I could not tie a bow. I would just tie knots in my shoelaces. So he sat me by the doorway and told me "You're not going back outside until you learn to tie your shoes." He went over the process with me repeatedly, attempting to teach me how to tie a bow. I think to this day I only tie half of the shoelace.

In school, I always thought it was normal that I didn't understand the work. I could not read textbooks, or do homework, but I bluffed my way through kindergarten and went on to first grade where I flunked. Can you believe it? Failing the first grade? I went to second grade with no idea how I'd gotten there, but somehow I managed to pass. Then, I went to the third grade, which I failed and had to do all over again. I was almost shaving by the time I got to fourth grade. Now at my adult age, I believe dyslexia comes in several different forms. One is rapid eye movement. The second is audio when you really don't hear words. The third is that the brain doesn't recognize sight or sound properly, so the end result is a severe learning disability. I can look at a word or a phone number a thousand times, and not be able to spell it or recall it.

   I did, however, join the grade school band where I studied percussion, drums, and cymbals. Perfect for a hyperactive person like myself. It was a real learning experience. Having to count and do the band music like Stephen Foster, learning to march in parades, and of course, having that perfect uniform, were all extremely challenging. I still had some trouble, because drumming must be precise. But I could not read the music, especially when the tempo was going fast. During rehearsals, which were held in the gymnasium, the conductor Otto Matee would always start pounding his baton on the music stand yelling, "Stop the band!" Of the fifty band members, he would pick on me because my timing of the cymbal crashing was off. He would berate me with terrible comments like "Don't you know how to count?" That wasn't the only problem. Whenever our band marched for parades, or performances, we were always out of step, and it was always my fault. I could never follow the normal way of marching, so like many other things in my life I just made my own way. I wish my guessing skills were better, because I was way off. My steps were the complete opposite of how I was supposed to be marching. I was just giving the conductor more reasons to pick on me.

Because of being dyslexic, my vision was impaired. I could not interpret the notes on the paper or concentrate. Normal people read from left to right, but in my case I have rapid eye movement. If you were looking at me, you would not see my eyes moving. It's a disconnection between the eye and the brain. I was playing cymbals that you crash together with both hands. I would always guess about where the crashes should be, and I was always wrong. That's when Otto would stop me. Looking back on my band years, we could have made a good comedy act called "The Dyslexic Cymbal Player and the Conductor."

In those days, no one knew about dyslexia, and learning disorders. They didn't know there was something wrong with you, you must've just been dumb. It was like putting a dunce cap on your head and sitting in the corner until the class was over. Do you remember when the teacher would ask the class "raise your hand if you know this answer"? Then the teacher would call on the person that did not raise their hand? That was me. It was always me. It was so embarrassing, and I would ask myself, "Why did she call on me? I didn't raise my hand!" There's a line from Jonathan Winters, the great comedian. He would say in one of his first records about a grade school student that was slow, "Ain't he dumb ain't he dumb! Oh don't raise your hand!" That's when a teacher would call on me, when I didn't have the answer. It seemed to me the girls were always smarter than the boys. Whenever they were called on, they always had the correct answer.

There was this one little Italian girl that sat next to me. She was very pretty. Her hair was long and as black as midnight, she had big brown eyes, and wore the prettiest dresses every day. She looked like she could have been my sister, but of course, she was not. I remember one day she had on a red dress. She was so beautiful. She would smile at me every day, and I would smile back. We met in the coat room one day. In those days we did not have lockers; there was just a large closet in back of the classroom where we would hang our coats. I remember that we were looking into each other's eyes, and then we kissed on the lips. It was my first kiss... Wow! What I remember most of all, was her garlic breath. It was my first experience with garlic. I never kissed a girl again until I was about 15 years old. She passed me a note once, but I couldn't read it. To this day I still don't know what it said. Just think, we were only in third grade but we probably could've spent the rest of our lives together making Italian meatballs with garlic.

I remember when I would walk home from school. No one was home, not mom, dad, or my brother. I was hungry, so I would eat soda crackers. Sometimes I would walk down the alley in search of food. You see everyone had a garden in their backyard, and I would look through the gardens for something to eat. I think deep inside of me I was looking for meatballs, but I didn't know if meatballs grew in gardens or not. So I picked something that looked like red celery and ate it. It turned out to be rhubarb. Man, was it sour! But I was hungry enough to eat it. You see, I was one of the first latch key kids, and I didn't even need a key - the door was always open.

When I was ten, my mother enrolled me in Northwestern Naval and Military Academy, for the summers. It was a form of being babysat, and taking studies at the same time. There was a beautiful landscaped yard at the school. It was a very large building. While I was there, I needed help with reading and spelling. My mother paid extra for a private tutor, for two hours a day. It was quite a culture shock. I would read from a book that he gave me, and while I was reading he would cringe and shake his head. I thought he had some kind of nervous condition, but he was getting paid to tutor me so he persevered. At every session he would shake his head just like that eye doctor.

It was an all-boys school, with the exception of the nurse, and she was hot! I would sometimes fake being sick, just to see her. Most of the kids there came from wealthy families from the Chicago area, but some came from other states. We had to wear uniforms, dress and casual, even though it was summer. We wore blue shorts, a white shirt, and sailor hat at all times. The kids who attended were well mannered. All had good haircuts, and good grammar. Not like the kids on my block who would say things like "ain't got none" instead of "don't have any." But there was still crime, and I was part of it. We would sneak into the downstairs kitchen in the middle of the night, past the watchman, using our flashlights to see, and steal sugar for Kool-Aid. Then we would sneak back up to our rooms, past the watchman again, and make Kool-Aid. That was our idea of high crime.

The kids at the school would always look forward to packages from their family. We would receive cookies, and treats. One roommate I had, he was from Kentucky, would receive chocolate covered ants in the mail. He was such a slob! Always spilling those gosh darn ants all over the floor. One day, an officer came in for a surprise inspection. I knew we were gonna get canned for the ants. No surprise, we were confined to our room for the weekend. No outside activities allowed. I was so angry with him, that I divided the room into sides. I laid out the rules very carefully for him "This is my side, that's your side. DON'T cross the line pal."

It was really different from my neighborhood, but I liked it. It was refreshing. I had my own dresser and bed, and I got along well with most of my roommates over the four summers I spent there. It was bittersweet. Although I was lonely, it was a beautiful place overlooking Lake Geneva, Wisconsin. Mom, and

Dad visited me once. My brother Sam, and his friends drove up to see me on occasion. Even Mr. Romano appeared unexpectedly to visit me. I wondered, why?

From my window I could see sailboats on the big lake. There were also powerboats, mostly Chris Craft, which are the most elegant boats I've ever laid eyes on. Lake Geneva had many powerboats, including several owned by Wrigley, one of which was the fastest boat on the lake. They had a distinct sound from the motor.

There was one instructor at the school called Bud. I don't know why he singled me out, but he would invite me on boat rides in the school's Chris Craft boat. That made me feel so special, getting to experience the clean air of the lake and the sound of the boat's motor. Normally, if I got to do anything, I was accompanied by several of the other students. Alone, I was able to really appreciate the experience.

Most of the students in my class were experienced in sports. Although Dad was so good to me, making sure I ate every day, he did not teach me to fish, play cards, or shoot hoops. I never learned any of those things. To this day I still have no idea how to play, or keep score in baseball, or football. Incidentally, today is October 31, 2016. The World Series is being played between the Chicago Cubs and Cleveland Indians. I have been watching a little bit of the game on the TV, but here I am at 71 years old and still don't know exactly how the game is played.

But it is very exciting! The Cubs have not won a World Series since 1908, and in 2016 that has all changed. The Cubs have won their first title in 108 years.

It was about 8th grade when my parents moved down the road, about a mile away. After that, I never got to see Richie anymore. He went to Catholic school, I went to the public school. We didn't see each other at school anymore either. My parents had the new house built, and it was a split-level. Very modern at the time. I soon met a new family next door. It was the Cappista family, of Italian descent. They had a kid named Lenny who was my age, and we became friends. I guess he replaced Richie.

I felt so comfortable being at their house, and being with Lenny. We looked alike. He had brown eyes, dark hair, and dark skin. His father was short, had dark skin, dark hair, and I believe his mother was Italian also. But the best part was the food, it was amazing! I could smell the garlic, and meatballs, all the way from our house next door.

I remember many times I would go over to their house, and just sit at their kitchen table. No one was home, but I would just sit there waiting. They took me in like family. One time Mr. Cappista came home, and saw me sitting at their kitchen table. He asked me "Are you waiting for Lenny?" I replied, "No, I'm waiting for everyone." He just shook his head and said "Okay."

Dad, with all his well-meaning heart, was cooking

German food with sauerkraut. Meanwhile, they were cooking next door with meat, tomato sauce, onions, and garlic. I just loved it. I now felt inside of my body, that my genes were telling me this was the food I had been searching for. I knew it in my heart.

Down the back alley from our new house, I got a job at a grocery store. I was only about 127 pounds, but there I was, with an apron on. I learned about produce, how to stack canned goods, and things about meats. I also learned to operate the cash register. One day, a guy came up to me and said, "Hey kid, I just gave you a ten dollar bill, but you only gave me change for a five." So I opened up the drawer and gave him his five dollars back. That night when my boss counted the till, turns out I was five dollars short. Since I was only making a dollar an hour, I had to work the next five hours for free. I didn't want this to happen again, so I came up with my first invention. I wired a small light into the cash register's drawer, on each cash latch, and it would blink on the last bill entered. I never made incorrect change again.

I liked doing carry-outs at the store, because I could walk out into the parking lot, and see all these beautiful cars. I would dream, "Someday I'll have one like that." But at a dollar an hour it was gonna take a while.

There were three brothers that owned the store, and it was called Sunkist grocery store. The brothers were from Greece, and they spoke the language. I even started learning some Greek that

John, the oldest, would teach me. I didn't find out until later that he was only teaching me bad words. The store was a great experience for me, and I met lots of people from all walks of life. I worked after school, and on the weekends.

    I was good at the job, but I did have a lot of trouble with reading the scale. I would weigh tomatoes, onions, and other vegetables in order to price them. After weighing them, I would put them in a little bag, and write the price on the bag with a marker. I would always guess. One time my boss came up to me and asked me, "What the hell are you doing?" I had charged $2 for just one small onion. Guess it was that dyslexia, again.

    One of the jobs I hated at the store was when these little Greek women would come in wearing babushkas, and ask for Greek olives. I would have to go to the back, put my hands into a barrel full of Greek olives, put the olives into a little container, and take it out to the customer. My fingers would get so cold from that barrel that they almost froze off! After that, I would run and hide whenever I saw a lady with a babushka on.

    We would also bag potatoes up by five pounds. That was finally easy to me. Just put the bag on the scale, and fill it with potatoes until the scale went up to five. One day my boss left me alone while bagging potatoes. I had every bag perfect, right on the five pound mark. My boss walked up to me after I had done about twenty bags, reached over, grabbed a bag of potatoes, put it on the scale and said to me, "Never put five pounds of potatoes in a five pound bag." Then he started taking one or two out of each bag. I learned that they never actually put five pounds of potatoes in a five pound bag. Now that I finally had something right, it turned out to be wrong.

As I mentioned, John, one of the owners, was teaching me to speak Greek. I did not know, however, that he was only teaching me swear words. I was so proud to learn how to say "How are you today?" in Greek, that I said it to an old Greek lady at the store. I asked her what I thought was, "How are you today?" But instead I had said, "You have a very big ass." She went right up to my other boss Jimmy, and told him what I said. Jimmy, John's brother, came out, grabbed me by the ear, and walked me over to John. He yelled at him "Dammit John, if you're going to teach this kid Greek, teach him the right words! He just told Mrs. Poulos, our good customer, that she has a fat ass!" From that day forward, John taught me the right words and phrases. To this day my ear still hurts!

One Christmas Eve, John and I were working late. At about 7 o'clock we were just getting ready to close, when the telephone rang. I answered, and the man asked me, "Do you have any Christmas trees left?" I looked outside, and saw there were two. One in bad shape, you could just see right through it. The other one was faring a little better, and wasn't too bad. The man on the phone said, "I just drove 500 miles. I haven't seen my wife for two months, and I want to bring her a Christmas tree. I'll be there in 10 minutes." We sat there and waited for the man. He showed up in a big Cadillac, and John told him "Back up your car." The man got out to look at the trees. I remember how cold, and snowy it was outside. We showed the man the two Christmas trees that we had left, and of course he picked the better of the two. John told the man "Go sit in your car its cold out here." It was cold. My ears were bright red, my fingertips like icicles, and my toes on the verge of frostbite. Even though I was frozen, I started to put the good tree in the trunk, but John stopped me and said, "No, kid, no. The other tree." So I did what I was told. I put the tree you could see right through in the guy's trunk. Can you imagine when the guy got home to his wife, and brought that tree in? She probably kicked him out for bringing home that Charlie Brown look-a-like tree. These are just some of the funny stories from the grocery store years. I loved all of the family members who owned the store, and the customers too. They were like an extended family to me. John, Jimmy, Nick, Tony, Teddy and Mary Dee. My memories of you will last forever.

    By grade school, I had been taking professional drum lessons for several years. Since I had discovered my talent for playing the drums, I joined a couple polka bands to make some extra money. Usually I would play on Saturday nights at weddings. Seeing these older people do the polka was always a trip. They were always drunk and making fools of themselves. If I never play *Roll out the Barrel* again, it'll be too soon. Although they never had any meatballs at the buffet.

Yes, I guess I had a full schedule. I was going to school, working at the grocery store, and playing in a band! It was mandatory back then that you had to join the musicians union, so I went and got my name in the book listed under drummers. After that, I started getting calls for drumming jobs. I started playing dinner shows with the bands, and we would also play at nightclubs. I was pretty young at the time to be playing the 21-year-old places with these great musicians. I learned a lot in that time. I also started doing standup comedy. It first happened at one wedding reception. We were playing music, and suddenly the photographer ran up and yelled, "Stop playing! We have to take pictures now of the bride and groom in front of the band." The bride was standing there in her beautiful wedding dress, but the groom was nowhere to be seen. I got off my drum stool, and grabbed the microphone to make an announcement: "Is there any male out there that will stand in for the groom for the wedding pictures?" The band started laughing, and so did the wedding guests. I then turned to the bride, still holding the microphone, and I said, "Do you want to pick out another handsome man to be in your wedding picture? Because we can't find the groom." The crowd continued to laugh. Finally the groom walked in from the bar, staggering drunk, with a red face and crooked tie, while I stood next to his new bride. I said one more time, "Are you sure you want him in your wedding picture?" Everyone laughed again. From then on I started doing standup whenever I could.

It was the summer of 1961 that I was a hired to play drums with some of musicians from the University of Illinois jazz band. They were really professional jazz cats. We were called the Chicago 5, and we got a job for the summer in northern Wisconsin in Fish Creek Door County. The club was called The Rock. I had to lie about my age, because you had to be 21 to get in. So I told everyone I was 22. The audience loved to listen to our music, and they would always dance; the place was packed every night. I was used to people dancing throughout my life in suits and ties, but never in bathing suits. It was quite interesting, playing at a summer resort. I can't remember if thongs were popular yet.

Musicians work about 40 minutes on stage, and 20 minutes off in one Saturday night. I went out for a break one night, because it was hot and sweaty in the club. The problem was, when I tried to go back in, I couldn't get back through the front door. There was a bouncer who asked for my ID. I told him, "I work inside. I'm the drummer in the band." He wouldn't budge. "I've heard that story before." He replied snottily. So I walked around the side of the building and found there was a window right above the stage. It was kind of high, so I tried yelling to the band inside. Instead I hear the announcer over the PA asking, "Where's the drummer?" They're inside getting ready to play and I'm stuck yelling from outside, "I'm here! I'm out here!" I almost got caught by security, but finally the band members heard my cries. They had to reach down, and pull me through the window by my arms. As my knees were scraping up the side of the building, I thought to myself "Lies always catch up with you." I never went outside for a break again, and I never lied about my age again. I made it through that summer, and even though I had an already busy life, I also took up some acting.

The theatrical group I joined was called the Peninsula Players. I did comedy acts for the opening routine. They were located down the street from the night club I worked at, on the shore in a very affluent area. There were beautiful summer homes on the peninsula, mostly owned by Chicago folks. They call the peninsula the Cape Cod of the Midwest. I did some sailing, and some Scuba diving while there. It was a wonderful summer. I remember one night even Mr. Romano showed up. He said to me that he was just driving through. I thought to myself, how do you drive through a peninsula? He took me out to dinner, and watched me play in the band. I think he was there at least two nights. He always showed up at the strangest times and places throughout my life. Why?

But eventually the season had to end. I packed up my drum set in the back of my Chevrolet convertible that I'd driven around all summer. I had purchased it before I left, with the money I made from the grocery store and my drumming jobs. When summer ended, I drove back to Illinois to start school again. I was about 16 or 17 at the time. While driving back, I thought about how bittersweet it was. Summertime is wonderful, going to the beach, and meeting new people. It's always sad when you have to leave. It reminds me of when I was younger, and had to go away to the military school. It's a lonely feeling. Afterwards I went back to how my life had been. Back to my parents' house, back to the grocery store, and back to weekend drumming jobs.

The Summer Wind ~ Frank Sinatra

KITTY AND THE ALY KATS

In 1964 I was 19 yrs. old I joined the band called Kitty and the Aly Kats it was a trio and I was the drummer. Lenny Perretta, was the owner of the band, and Charlene Oliver was the singer and dancer. So we made up the band Kitty and the Aly Kats. Lenny was an extremely talented musician, and singer. His voice was reminiscent of Perry Como and Frank Sinatra. He played what was known as the cordovox. It's an accordion best for jazz music, one of the newest versions of the times. His skills rivaled Dick Contino and Art Van Damme. It had all the features of a big pipe organ. With just the click of a button you could have any sound you want; piano, sax, trumpet... Man, those cats played.

Lenny wore the straps over him like an accordion. The cordovox was extremely heavy. He played the bass in his left-hand, which kept the rhythm going in the band. Even though there were only two musicians in the band, Lenny's accordion made it sound like a 20 piece orchestra. Man did we swing! Charlene was a marvelous singer, and wore great costumes. They were very intricate dresses, with beading and a unique shine. She and Lenny would sing duets, and solos with harmony in the background. We really had a great show band.

We were doing things like Route 66, a shuffle beat for the drums. If you ever heard Louis Prima, Keely Smith, or

Manhattan Transfer, that was the sound of our band. The audience was just amazed at our show. Yes, we were doing shows. We were a show band. We traveled the Midwest for several months, only stopping in towns for about two weeks at a time. We played VFW clubs, American Legion halls, and being a show band, we did a lot of dinner club shows.

One club I remember, in Waukegan Illinois, was a first-class place. It had a great stage, lighting system, a live light man, and beautiful sound system. Booths, chairs and tables faced the stage. It's ideal for musicians, especially doing a show. We did two shows a night, and the audience was always packed. The room was similar to the Playboy club, which I had worked a few years before joining the Aly Kats.

One night while on break I was walking around the room, and I saw the strangest thing. Patrons of the club would walk up the staircase, and knock on a wall. To my amazement, a little door opened to see who was knocking, and then the wall itself would open up to let people in. I decided to go knock on the wall. The little door slid open, and a guy let me in. All of the sudden it felt like I'd been sent back in time to the 1920's. This secret club was like a modern day speakeasy. Inside there were over 100 people. Smoke filled the room, and it looked to me like a Las Vegas casino. There were green felted card tables, roulette wheels, and craps. Lively jazz music played in the background, and everyone in the room was dressed to the nines. The dealers were all dressed in classic 20's fashion. The men sporting tuxedos, and the women in flapper gowns. Before I could take it all in, a heavy set bouncer, with a collar so tight it couldn't button, came up to me and said "Hey kid, you don't belong here! Go back in the other room where you belong, and don' tell the coppers." I could hardly understand his slurred words. But I left without causing a ruckus.

I couldn't believe this amazing place was just on the other side of the wall. To think, I'd been playing there for a week and never even knew it was there! It was amazing that you couldn't hear the sounds through the wall. I was only 17, and there I was working in an adult world. The rest of the time I played, I could only look at the wall. I would watch people come and go, and imagine the crime going on inside. Would the club be raided? I just hoped we wouldn't be caught in the middle. I never did tell Lenny, or Kitty what I saw.

There was also this one time we played in Minnesota, in a town called New Ulm. It was like being in Germany. They had German breweries, which employed most of the town. There were hills in the background, and it felt like you weren't even in the United States. It was amazing. We were treated like celebrities everywhere we went. People wanted us to come to their homes for dinner, and sign autographs. There were no meatballs in New Ulm, just Sauerkraut!

Our agent, Eddie Hall, would book us these jobs for two

weeks, hoping we would be discovered like all musicians waiting for that big break. During the month of May, in 1964, we had a gig at the American Legion club in Fargo, North Dakota. Believe it or not a lot of celebrity musicians played at the Legions. It was a steppingstone to being well known. In fact, I understand Herb Alpert was there the week before we started, and was paid $125 a week. About that time he created the record company A & M. Shortly after that, he made $100,000,000 in one year with his band called Herb Alpert and the Tijuana Brass.

Bubbles, Bangles, and Beads ~ Frank Sinatra

THE BREAKFAST COUNTER

I had a room at the Fargo Hotel, and of course being a musician living in hotels you had to go out for your breakfast, lunch and dinner. One morning I went down to the hotel restaurant, and sat at the counter. That was the day my life changed. It was May 3, 1964. Sitting at the counter across from me was the most beautiful woman I've ever seen in my entire life. I had been traveling and on stage looking at hundreds and hundreds of people in the audience. Never ever had I seen anyone so beautiful. She had long black hair, and olive colored skin. She looked just like Sophia Loren. We made eye contact, and she immediately introduced herself as Cynthia. Her father George had a rug company next door to the hotel. They were of the Lebanese decent. The next thing I knew, I was at her father's company being introduced to her family. I guess I fell in love with not only her, but her whole family.

Her dad would work many hours at the store selling carpeting. It reminded me of my mother and her beauty shop. Her father was very well known in Fargo, and he had been selling rugs and carpeting for many years. George was also heavily involved with the local community theater, and had not so long ago directed a play that was one of Dustin Hoffman's first plays. This was a few years before his role in the *Graduate* with Anne Bancroft.

Cynthia had a younger sister, Stephanie, and an older brother DeLayne who was a bookworm. The guy was about 300 pounds, and all he would do was read. He spoke four languages, and was a professional student all his life. DeLayne had all kinds of degrees, but had a hard time talking to people because he was so smart. He would always wear a suit with a shirt and clip on bow tie, for he was so smart he couldn't tie a regular tie. Man, he was a trip.

Cynthia's mother Hazel was absolutely bizarre. She would spend the whole morning putting on makeup, in front of her vanity. She always wore a poncho, and held a cigarette in her hand. Her clothes would always smell of smoke. It would be almost noon, and she would call George for a ride. Then George would have to come pick her up when he was in the middle of selling carpeting, and talking with customers. It was a real inconvenience to George. He'd have to close the store for almost 20 minutes to go pick up Hazel. His son DeLayne couldn't drive, so George would have to pick him up later. Then, they would all meet every day at the restaurant hotel next door for lunch. After ordering lunch, DeLayne would go to the book carousel, and read a book. He would literally read a whole book in about three minutes, while his eggs were being made, then come and sit with us, clear his throat several times and say, "I just read the most interesting book." During lunch he would actually tell us the story from beginning to end.

My two weeks were almost up at the American Legion club. I felt like a soldier meeting someone on leave, and having to go back to the army. Cynthia and I spent every day together during that time, and we both knew I only had hours before we packed up our instruments, and left town. Well, to make a short story long, after leaving Fargo and going to other gigs around Midwest, we must have run up hundreds and hundreds of dollars in phone bills. Poor George not only had to pay for Hazel's make- up and cigarettes, and DeLayne's books, now Cynthia's long distance phone bills.

Just weeks after I went back with the band we missed each other so much I drove 750 miles to see her again, and we eloped. Even though her bedroom was on the second floor we didn't use a ladder. She snuck out the back door. I was too young to get married in any other state so we drove my sports car to Clarksville, Tennessee. This was a southern town, and it was very hot. We checked into a hotel and went through the process of getting married with a justice of the peace. He was an old southern gentleman, who wore a white suit and a string bow tie. He looked just like Col. Sanders.

There we were married. That was when we started disagreeing about everything. We argued every day, several times. She moved back to her parents' house in Fargo, and I got fired from Kitty and the Aly Kats. Our agent Eddie watched some of our shows, and decided he wanted to replace me with a drummer that could sing and do harmony with Charlene and Lenny. Later, Charlene went to work with a famous band leader Ray Anthony, and traveled the world for the next twenty years.

I was back at my parents' house without a job, and married to a lady that's living in her parents' house in Fargo North Dakota, approximately 750 miles away. I couldn't stop thinking of the day I met her at the counter. She was beautiful. I decided to drive up to Fargo to see her, and ended up spending a week. Needless to say, she got pregnant. On February 27, 1965, my daughter Tiffani was born. She was absolutely beautiful. While I was there, I was lucky enough to get a job playing drums in the Ward Dunkirk trio. It was in Moorhead, Minnesota, just three minutes from Fargo.

Ward was an accomplished musician. He played piano, and sang beautifully. He was in the original band with Bobby Vee. Bobby Vee became popular overnight when the plane crashed of Buddy Holly and Richie Valens. I've worked with Bobby on several occasions, after meeting him. Ward would pack the room every night. I got a little apartment in the area, and tried to get Cynthia to move into it with me. She, however, preferred to stay in her parents' house a few blocks away. We argued every day that we talked.

Leaving on a Jet Plane ~ John Denver

YOUR FATHER'S MUSTACHE

It was the year 1968. I was working on stage at a ski resort in Alpine Valley, Wisconsin, outside of Lake Geneva. I was performing, not at the main amphitheater, but at a smaller venue inside the ski lodge. I was doing stand-up at the time. You may have heard of Alpine Valley before. Stevie Ray Vaughan, the famous guitarist, was killed after a concert there in a plane crash on August, 27 1990.

 A gentleman approached me one night there, by the name of Bob McKenzie. He was a tall, handsome man, with a heavy Boston accent, and dark circles that sat beneath his eyes. Bob said he was a talent agent for a company called Your Father's Mustache; a chain of banjo nightclubs. He liked my performance as a drummer, as well as my comedy act. He told me there was an opening for, believe it or not, a washboard player. I said "A washboard player? What am I going to do laundry, or am I going to work in the band?"
"No, that's one of the main instruments in a banjo band" He then gave me a record to listen to, and study. It was one of the Your Father's Mustache records. Bob said he would call me about a week later to see if I was interested in joining. I studied the rhythms of the washboard player endlessly.

 I got the job, and my mother told me I should call Dominic, to let him know I was leaving for a job out of state. I wondered what concern it was of his. Regardless, I went to his house. It was a big Victorian house on a hill, and by that time, he'd had his other leg amputated. As I walked in, he was "standing" in the parlor. The backs of his dining room chairs were lined up on either side, and he used them to support himself on his prosthetic legs. He was forcing himself to walk. I was amazed at his determination. Dominic was always a tough guy, and he was determined to walk however he could. It was so heartbreaking that he was forced to live in a wheelchair.

Dominic had a housekeeper named Guy, who was a drunk, and lived above the coach house in the back. When Dominic needed him, he would ring a hand bell, and Guy would sometimes appear. Guy would drive him to his office every day. Dominic was a workaholic, and not even his legs could stop him. The technology for today's amputees is much better than it was back then. All the soldiers coming home from the war now can, for the most part, live a normal life.

In February of 1968, I was on a plane headed to New Orleans for Mardi Gras, to play at a Your Father's Mustache club. There I was flying to New Orleans for the first time, to join a banjo band playing washboard. I found the club was located at the heart of Bourbon Street. Beforehand I had some free time, so I visited the famous Court of the Sisters, and Pat O'Brien's Blacksmith Shop. At Pat's I spent some time drinking with Jim Garrison, the prosecutor on the Oswald case, and Paul Hornung, the famous Green Bay running back. I was amazed at the famous people I'd met, and only on my first day in New Orleans. We were having a good time at the bar, and they invited me to their private club. It was located in the French Quarter, and was very nice, old authentic French.

The voices of New Orleans natives are just fantastic. Think about the voices of Louis Armstrong, The Neville Brothers, and Harry Connick Junior. They just have a great sound. I was quite welcome in the French Quarter. I went to so many other famous places in New Orleans, including the Metairie cemetery, which is famous for burying people above ground.

At the court of the two sisters, I recognized one of the piano players as my old musician's union president's daughter from Joliet. 'Gee' I thought 'I hope my union dues are paid.' That guy was always chasing me around for union dues, when I was playing jazz drums around Chicago. He would go around to all the clubs, and walk up on stage to make sure that union dues were paid. Literally, while we were playing. He would stand there and hold out his hand with his little book to mark paid if you paid. I wonder if a washboard is considered an instrument. If it is, I better look out for that union guy!

New Orleans is quite unique. There's lots of horses, and French accents, why they call it the French Quarter after all. There's also Preservation Hall. I should've sat in there one night when I had the chance, but sadly I didn't. Man, it really was a town of rhythm!

Then it was time to go to work.
When I first walked into the Y.F.M. Club, it looked like a step back in time to the roaring twenties. I met the manager Roger K, and started a few rehearsals with the band. I wore a period appropriate bathing suit as my costume. I would walk to work in that bathing suit, because the weather was so nice. People in New Orleans dressed in wild costumes during Mardi Gras, but I still got comments every night on the street like, "Where's the beach?" I would answer back "Where's the feather show?" There were a lot of feathers and jewelry during Mardi Gras. Even the customers at Y.F.M. wore costumes. Y.F.M. sold straw hats, and little mustaches that customer's would put underneath their nose, in an attempt to look like a dapper 20's gentleman. The place was always packed, and the room could hold about 400 people. We did four shows a night during Mardi Gras.

Joel, the owner and music director, had musicians from the other Mustache clubs across the country come in just for that week. We actually had four bands playing morning, noon, and night. It was non-stop for 16 hours a day during Mardi Gras. My ears were always ringing! Do you have any idea what it's like to have a trombone blasting in your ear for four to eight hours a day? Plus the tuba, and the banjos. I had a headache for about a year! Not just from the music, and crowd, but from the scratching of my washboard. Where's the drum? Even the crash of a loud symbol would have been a welcome sound.

Peanuts were always on the floor. People were always drinking beer, and man did they drink the beer. They drank it by the pitcher, and I mean the pitcher. The mug's there were the world's only left handed mustache mugs. You can still find some on eBay. I never saw so many drunks in my life at one time. I thought Chicago had drunks, after all Al Capone was a bootlegger there. But Y.F.M. didn't even serve food, just peanuts. One night there was a man that I recognized from Joliet, dancing on a table. He had to be in his late seventies, and was dressed in an authentic WWI uniform, complete with helmet. Turns out, he was my neighbor in Joliet that lived next to the grocery store where I worked as a kid. I couldn't believe it. He was one of the only living soldiers left from World War I, and was a runner-up for being on a United States postage stamp. I don't know if he lived long after that night. He drank pitchers of beer, and then danced all over tabletops. The band never stopped playing.

I got introduced to a lot of 20s music in that time, some of which originated in New Orleans. The banjo player, tuba player, and trombone player in the band were all fine musicians. I'd never played with a banjo player before, and now I was playing with two. I had a hard time at first, trying to get the sound of the rhythm. Of course it was my job to smile and keep the rhythm on the washboard. There was no piano, or drum set. Not even a string bass. The banjo band was nothing like a jazz trio, but I fell into the groove almost immediately. The audience loved everything we did. A lot of it was sing-alongs, with the words written on the walls of the club. There were WC Fields pictures that lined the walls of the club. Charlie Chaplin, The Three Stooges; that sort of thing. We played songs from the movies during that period of time. There I was, not playing jazz drums, but playing on a washboard which I'd built myself. It had a bicycle horn on it, pie pan, and a bell. I used thimbles on my fingers, and sometimes even spoons. From having taken drum lessons, I learned tempo 3/4, 4/4, 2/4, drum rolls, and accents. Now I incorporated all those skills into my fingertips. I even sang a song every night called *Mama Don't Allow!* If Buddy Rich, who I once took a drum lesson from, could just see me now. Or my idols Dave Brubeck, and Joe Morello. Remember they did that tune *Take Five*. Also my old grade school band teacher, Otto Mate, and in later years Bill Mueller, my drum teacher who played the Palmer House in Chicago for years. Yes, it was a lot different than playing with drum sticks. I would go to a manicurist with my thimbles on, and say "Please give me a shine."

    The waiters, bartenders, and all the other staff were total professional drunks. Well there were a few that weren't, but they all did a good job nonetheless. It was there that I met Joel Shivone. Joel was the owner of Y.F.M. He was a millionaire from Connecticut, and owned about 10 of these clubs. He also played banjo. Joel would travel from club to club playing banjo, working endlessly, and always managing reports. In spite of some time zone differences between the clubs across the country. The guy would just work, work, and work. One time the Y.F.M. band played the White House for President Johnson. Joel, in a hurry, had forgotten his shoes. It was quite a sight. He couldn't introduce a song on stage to save his life, because of his stutter, but he really could sing. As it turns out, he just did the Carnegie Hall concert reunion in 2014. I guess he's still playing banjo.

I was there for two weeks during the Mardi Gras time in New Orleans. As a jazz lover, I went to see Pete Fountain, the famous clarinet player, and also Al Hurt down the street. In addition to that, I also saw the hottest group around; Herb Alpert and the Tijuana Brass. I spent some time with Herb. As you know, he owned A&M records. There I was, surrounded by some of the largest producers in the world, working Bourbon St. playing the washboard. One night at the Roosevelt Hotel, I got to sit in playing drums with the lounge group. Herb was there, and he complimented me. God, to think I could've been Karen Carpenter.

After Mardi Gras, I was on my way to Miami Beach to the Jackie Gleason club at the Conrad Hilton Plaza. The Hilton Plaza gave Jackie Gleason $1,000,000 to front the room, and extra to design the room. It was a roaring twenties theme, and he named the room Joe the Bartender's. What was the best choice for entertainment? The Y.F.M. show band, of course. I remember I arrived in Miami. It was about 9 o'clock at night, but still warmer than New Orleans. I took a cab over to the Hilton, and headed into Joe the Bartender's. It was a first-class place, and there was even a dress code. As I was standing there to enter the room, the maître d' said to me "Can I help you?"

"Yes" I said "I'm here with the band, I'll be taking the washboard player's place." The maître d' then firmly said to me "You're not getting into this room until you put a tie on." He ordered me to go to the washroom, where there was an attendant who rented out ties for $3 apiece. All of his ties were very loud. If you were in the audience, and had rented a tie from him, it would stand out. If you didn't return the tie, he would keep your $3. About that time, fashion was changing for men. It was becoming accepted now to wear just a white turtleneck, and a blazer. This was not acceptable at Joe the Bartender's. I went in the bathroom and rented this very loud tie. You know turtlenecks do not have a collar, so I had to wrap the tie around my neck. When I finally got into the room, everyone was staring at me and the loud tie hanging around my neck. I looked over at the bar, there was still a bar even though it was a formal show lounge, and there was Soupy Sales. I don't know how he got in without a tie, but he was wearing a white turtleneck with a double-breasted blue blazer, same as I'd been. I noticed he wasn't wearing socks either. This was the first time I'd ever seen penny loafers worn without socks, especially in February. But it was Miami, not Chicago. I thought it was quite funny, and soon he started commenting on my tie, because he thought that it was quite funny.

While I was there I watched the last show, and then met the band. Being as I was there to take Joe Terra's place, I wanted to sit down with him. He was a New Yorker, and he also worked at the New York Club. The guy was a very talented washboard player, which might sound funny, but he had all sorts of bells and whistles, and he dressed like a clown every night. He even wore the same type of pigment around his eyes. Being as he was an Italian from New York, we got along real well. He commented on the tie around my turtleneck. Joe was a very funny guy, he just didn't like Miami Beach, and wanted to get back. He was homesick for the village.

Banu Gibson was the singer, and show leader at that club. She was very talented, and did well for herself. To this day, she is a headliner in New Orleans.

There was this one banjo player, I forgot his name but he was a very good looking kid, who happened to be a very talented pool player. Jackie Gleason had him over to his house on several occasions, to play pool. Gleason had starred in the movie *Minnesota Fats* about pool hustlers. He was by far an accomplished pool player, and made all of his own shots during filming. His costar, Paul Newman, had a stand in.

Y.F.M. had an apartment set up for the band to share. I

was still tired because Mardi Gras was extremely exhausting. I remember Joe Terra showing me how to run the siren. Yes, there was a siren on stage. It was connected to a 12 volt battery just like a car, and you would push a button with your foot to set it off. When the siren went off, that's when the curtains would open up for us to take the stage. It was very loud, like having a fire truck inside the room. Once a week, I had to go to the gas station down the street, on Collins Avenue, to get the battery recharged. I didn't have a car to put the battery in, so I would walk five blocks to the gas station to get the battery recharged. I would walk right past the Fountain Blue on Collins Avenue, and up on the marquee there was Frank Sinatra. He was in town filming *Lady in Cement,* an excellent movie. The cast would come into the club often. In fact, they said they were going to cast me as a Puerto Rican cab driver. At that time, a lot of Puerto Ricans were coming into South Miami, and there was an opening for a part as a cab driver. I had a little bit of a tan, was short, and had black hair so I decided to try out. For the scene, I'm driving the cab when Sinatra jumps in back. When I auditioned, it wasn't actually him, it was his double. I turn and say "Where to sir?" and he says "The Fountain Blue." I didn't get the part because I didn't have an authentic accent. Believe it or not, they actually took an authentic Puerto Rican off the streets, and cast him in a movie with Frank Sinatra. I bet he didn't even know who Frank Sinatra was. At least I had my chance. They also wanted Sonny, the trombone player, to do a small part. I don't believe he got it either.

There I was, walking up and down the street past the Fountain Blue, carrying a battery. Have you ever carried a battery? Then you'd know that there can be issues with acid. After about two weeks, all my shirts and pants had holes in them. The banjo player and his wife, who I was living with at the time, would do my laundry. When it came out in rags, she'd hold them up and ask "What have you been doing? Where did you buy these clothes?" She told me to take them back, and I told her it was from getting the battery recharged. I don't know how Joe Terra did it. My one shirt got quite a bit of attention. There was a breakfast counter in the hotel that I frequented. I would meet almost every morning with John Gary, and Diahann Carroll, and they would always mention the holes in my shirt. Diahann was doing a television show up stairs with Woody Allen on the John Gary Show.

Woody Allen was often in attendance at our shows, at Joe the Bartender's. I remember one night Woody called me over and said "Would you like to go for a ride downtown?" I said sure, and so we jumped in a cab with his manager and headed off. In downtown Miami, at about two in the morning we went by a newsstand. He wanted to buy a book, but when we got there he said "Look! I know that girl!" It was a picture of a lady on a magazine cover. Woody jumped out of the cab, and he bought all the copies of the magazine that were on the stand. He then proceeded to ask the owner if he had any more in the back. The guy said "Yeah, about three boxes." Woody bought all of them, put them in the cab, and then we took the drive back to my hotel, where they dropped me off. I met Woody Allen in 1968, and later spent time with him in New York at the Y.F.M. club. He played clarinet, and would frequently come and sit with the band.

My friend John Beck, from Joliet, was in a movie with Woody Allen called *Sleeper*. John had gone to California in 1965, and did a lot of commercials where we occasionally crossed paths. I had met Woody Allen five years before him and John filmed *Sleeper*.

Back to my story. The three of us would have breakfast almost every morning. They would find time to come downstairs and see our show at Joe the Bartender's. They loved everyone in the band. One night, Victor Borge was even in the audience to watch the show. Victor Borge, remember him? Funny guy. In his personal act, he would come in and play music upside down. He was on the Dean Martin Show several times.

The show band was the best of all the musicians. Each club had about four bands, so there were literally hundreds of musicians that worked for Y.F.M. clubs. There were trombone players, and tuba players, but the most prevalent were the banjo players. People called it a sing-along nightclub. The catchphrase was "The time of your life, is right under your nose!" Which referred to a beer. They sold more pitchers of Schlitz draft beer, than anywhere else in the world. The time of my life that I spent working at the Gleason club, was beyond words. The Show musicians were the best. There was a spotlight man, and the stage spun around when we started playing. The light man would follow the dancers in their costumes, and their steps while they danced, and sang. Joe the Bartender's room was in the downstairs of the Conrad Plaza, and upstairs there was a big ballroom where you could find a gentleman by the name of John Gary. He was an Irish tenor singer, and had a television show upstairs in the big auditorium. It was a national show, so everyone was coming down to make an appearance. I got to work with many people like Soupy Sales, Anthony Newly, Woody Allen, and even Colonel Sanders of Kentucky Fried Chicken fame. Colonel Sanders was even in our audience one night, all dressed up. He looked like he should have been part of the band. His attire included a small bow tie, striped vest, and he was all dressed in white. The list goes on of who would come into that room, including Gleason himself once a week to see the show.

    Our trombone player was Sonny Helmer. Sonny's playing is just one of the best memories of my life. He really played so beautifully. Sonny was a showman, even though he weighed almost 300 pounds. He would stand on one foot, take a sock off the other, and play the trombone slide with his bare foot! One foot, and yet he could play so beautifully that he captivated the crowd. They roared, and clapped every night. The Jackie Gleason Club will always be in my memories.

In the summer of 68', I went from Miami to the Cape Cod Y.F.M. club. Bob McKenzie put me up in a beach cottage on Nantucket Sound, in Cape Cod Dennis Port that his parents owned. Now I had this beach cottage, and I was working four hours a night at the mustache about a mile away. I drove a 1965 Austin Healey 3000 convertible. Cynthia and the kids came to Cape Cod for two weeks, and it was good to be with them. The beach was just across the way, and I frequently took them there. A fellow across the street rented small sailboats, and I would go sailing with him almost every day. We would sail east, in what I remember to be a Sunfish, and have lunch at a place called Thompson's Clam Bar. Then we would head west, and go by the Kennedy's compound. It was good, but soon Cynthia was ready to return back to her parents' house. We never sailed to Nantucket or Martha's Vineyard, but of course I've taken the ferry there. In fact, the Mustache band even played on the boat heading to Nantucket a couple of times. Other times, the Mustache band would ride around Cape Cod on top of a fire truck playing music. That was to promote the business. Joel had a fire truck in almost every city; New York, Boston, New Orleans, Chicago, etc. The Cape Cod cottage I was staying in had a little fireplace, which I lit every night to get the chill out from the salt air. It was the coziest place in the world, and I would fall asleep to the sound of ocean waves.

It really was a most magnificent summer! I began to do three nights a week in the Cape Cod Club, and three nights a week in the Boston Club, every week. Again, I felt a connection. It was like an Italian connection; there were a lot of Italians in the audience in Boston every night. When I heard that Boston accent, I just got that feeling from inside of me that I was Italian. I truly believe I should've been born and raised in Boston, especially around the old North Church.

The Mustache band eventually did a concert for St. Christopher's Day in Boston. I was on stage with the priest, and mayor of Italian ceremonies. Looking out into the audience, there were literally a couple thousand Italians. What a privilege! There goes those genes again.

Every night I would look into the audience while I was performing in Boston, and it felt like I was seeing brothers, sisters, cousins, aunts, and uncles that I never had. It felt like it was a house with meatballs.

The following summer I continued working the Boston and Cape Cod clubs, traveling back and forth. I eventually made my way to the New York Club. Working in New York, the band did many outside jobs, including working the 1969 World Series between the Mets and the Orioles. We would go out to the ballpark every day, and play music in a little entertainment area.

On Sunday nights we even got to go down to the Ed

Sullivan Theater, and do warm-ups for the audience before the main show. The Mustache show band appeared several times live on the Ed Sullivan Show.

Back in 68' we also rehearsed for an upcoming tour playing college concerts. We had just finished a concert at the University of Iowa in the early evening, and were flying back that night to play the Chicago Club. The night before, martin Luther King Jr had been shot in Memphis. Getting to the airport in Ohio was fine, but once we got to the Chicago airport there were riots. Police cars everywhere, and taxicab's with taped up windows, so the glass wouldn't shatter when rocks came flying in. As we got off the plane we weren't sure what was going on, and we had a hell of a time getting from the O'Hare Airport to the downtown Chicago Club. Rocks were been thrown from overpasses, windows were shattered up and down State Street, and the windows at the club were broken too. We didn't perform that night. Eventually, we went back to the airport where people were still throwing rocks. We finally got back to New York, and spent the night there. The Chicago Club was closed.

As I said, I was with the show band, getting ready to do college concerts across the country. We rehearsed in a downtown studio in New York City where, I still have a picture of Pat Boone because once he was in the building rehearsing, and he walked over to say hello. I think it's funny because I credit myself with taking the world's first selfie, when we took that picture. I wanted to be in the picture along with everyone, so I pointed the camera at the mirror. It reflected back and got everybody in our group, Pat Boone included! So I am credited, in my own mind, with taking the first selfie ever. Again we set off to college concerts, which were always big crowds, in big auditoriums full of students.

Sonny Helmer eventually left the band. After Y.F.M. he went to Disney World, and Disneyland. He played both venues for a while. I visited one time in California years later, and saw his act. He's retired now, and has a book out; *Everything Happens to Me! The Almost Famous Sonny Helmer Story.*

I stopped and visited him in Atlanta a couple years ago in October of 2015, when I drove from Chicago to Naples, Florida. He looked good, and had lost a lot of weight. Sonny was currently living in a retirement home. In his room there, he still plays the trumpet and electric keyboard. Sadly, he stopped playing trombone, because it wasn't an instrument that was made to be heard solo. However, he could play both the keyboard and trumpet at the same time, one hand each. His trombone still hangs on his wall behind him. So many good memories with him. It's just amazing when you're on stage with such talent. When there's real talent, the music is not only incredible, but you have the opportunity to work with so many great people.

We worked with Dave Garroway once. We did the television show *The Dave Garroway Show* in Boston, in 1969.

The guests that day were The Mustache Band, Walter Brennan, and Ed Wynn. I had a long talk with Walter Brennan, who was in hundreds of films, including the movie *To Have and Have not* where he starred alongside Humphrey Bogart. Believe it or not, I can't remember if he actually had a limp.

We also worked with Orson Bean around the same time. While I was with the New York Band, we were hired by Mayor Lindsay's reelection campaign in 1969. We played at stops along his campaign trail, and pulled the fire truck trick again. Except this time it was to promote a candidate, not a club.

One time we were playing on the steps of the John Hancock building for a campaign event, and Orson Bean was there to give a speech. I met him afterwards, talked to him, and thought he was a brilliant man. It was just unbelievable, all these celebrities I got to work with, and their work was so genius. Woody Allen, Walter Brennan, Anthony Newly... The list goes on and on.

We also worked with Jesse Owens the Olympic track star, Byron Nelson the golfer, and Chris Schenkel the famous sportscaster. I met Chris and Jesse while playing at a sales convention in Rhode Island. Jesse taught me how to eat lobster while we were together, and Chris seemed to have a photographic memory. He came and talked to the band, and afterwards he would remember every single person's name, and say goodbye to each person. I suppose that come from having to remember all the player's names. I still keep in communications with a few of the mustache managers and musicians, through social media. We all feel that there is a hole in our lives, because it was such a great time. In fact, about a year ago there was a reunion of Your Father's Mustache at Carnegie Hall. I wasn't aware of it, or I would've attended. There were about fifty or sixty old, and I mean *old,* musicians all there to play. It's all on YouTube if you want to go watch. They all played in the nightclubs of Your Father's Mustache 40 years ago, and now they're playing at Carnegie Hall. I wish I would've known.

The end of the Mustache nightclubs was due to the rise of disco. Disco, karaoke, and rock was now being played in nightclubs. Before we closed in Boston, our club was below the Improper Bostonian, which many remember to this day.

Soon clubs started closing one at a time, and even though it had to end it was one of the best times of my life. I must say from the bottom of my heart, thank you to all I met and worked with. Joel, you are b-b-b-beautiful. Bob McKenzie, thank you for finding me. Sonny, Banu, and Harry, you all went on to do great things. Thank you to so many other musicians, waiters, managers, and finally Harry Lip Productions; where the time of my life, was right under my nose!

As for me, I got word that Cynthia had finally, after all these years, moved into her own apartment with the kids, just a few blocks from her parents. I had a decision to make. Do I continue to work in the New York Club that's still open in Greenwich Village, where I had an apartment around the corner, and in show business working with famous people? Or do I move back with Cynthia and the kids, who were three, and five years old by now. Cynthia would not move to New York with me. I made the decision to pack my bags, and leave Greenwich Village. I flew to Fargo immediately to be with Cynthia and the kids, where she had invited me to live with her.

When you are Smiling ~ Louis Prima and Keely Smith

THE MAILBOX

I'd been back in Fargo, in Cynthia's apartment for about a week now, and I was getting settled in. It was so nice to be with the kids again. It was late morning, and Cynthia had left with the kids for the park. I had to mail back the Y.F.M. Company credit card, and some receipts to New York. I addressed the envelope to Your Father's Mustache 7th ave. New York, NY, then proceeded to walk about a block and a half to the mailbox. Once I was there, I put the envelope into the box, and headed back home.

There was a sheriff deputy waiting in the hallway, when I arrived back at the apartment. He asked if I was Vincent Herr. I told him I was, and he said "I'm here to serve you with divorce papers." I was perplexed, and could only reply with "Oh there must be some mistake. I just came back from New York to live with my family, with my wife and kids. We've been planning this for several weeks."
"Well the papers are dated from this morning, just about an hour ago. You have to leave premises, and leave the keys with me." He regretfully told me.
"Okay, but can I get my things?"
"What do you have?"
"Just my clothes, toothbrush, and razor." He agreed, and accompanied me into the apartment. I gathered my things into

the two suitcases I had, which only a week before, I'd unpacked from New York. As I walked out the door, I looked back and saw the kid's toys. Suddenly I felt all alone. Abandoned.

There I was, standing outside the apartment with two suitcases, no car, no idea where I'm going to stay, and getting choked up in the middle of the day. I thought I better go to the bank, and get some money. It was 1970 and the style for men, at least in New York, was bell bottom pants, and a flowered shirt, so that was my attire. I walked to a phone booth, and called a taxi cab, which I was so used to doing in New York. I arrived at the bank, went up to the teller, and wrote a check for $25. Back then, that felt like $100 would today. I had one of those temporary checks, for I had just opened the account a few days before. She looked at my account, and said "I'm sorry Sir, I cannot cash this check." Again I was shocked, first I was kicked out, now I can't get any money? "Well it's a new account, maybe you don't have the paperwork yet." I said to her, hoping to change the situation. It didn't help, and she sent me over to the bank manager. The man was sitting at a desk in the middle of the lobby, like a fresh out of school newbie. Not even a week ago, when I opened the account, I was invited to the chief bank manager's office, which was behind a glass partition. This time, I was just sitting in the lobby, talking to a young bank person. He looked up and said to me "Well the account's been frozen." I said "Frozen? I just opened the account!" At this point it was overwhelming. He told me he understood that the sheriff dropped off papers this morning, and apparently my account was tied up in the court system because of the divorce.

There I was again. Alone, sitting in the bank lobby with two suitcases, bell bottom pants, a flowered shirt, and no money. People were staring at me. I bet they were thinking I was making a large deposit, or something. I only had $15 to get a hotel room with, but that was a problem because they were usually between $40 and $70 a night. I thought to myself, maybe I can get my credit card back. I decided to take a cab back to the mailbox.

When I arrived, I said to the cabbie "Wait here for me, I have to get something out of the mailbox." He looked suspicious, and questioned "You're not gonna steal mail are you?" I told him no. I went over, opened the mailbox lid, and reached my hand down inside in an attempt to retrieve my envelope. I could feel it with the tips of my fingers, but I just couldn't grasp it. I decided to jump a little bit, in an attempt to reach farther down. That was a mistake. Next thing I knew, my arm was stuck, lodged at the elbow! My feet were off the ground, and I was left dangling. I yelled to the cab driver "Help me, help me please!" He quickly ran over, and tried to free my arm, but his attempt failed. He went, found a big rock, and put it underneath my feet. I was glad, because it relieved some of the pressure on my elbow. Then he went back to his cab, and used his radio to call for an ambulance.

When they arrived, the first paramedic asked "Are you

stealing mail?" I told him "No. I mailed the letter earlier. I need to get it back." They also tried to get my arm out, but to no avail. Their solution was to call the postmaster, so he could unlock the bottom door, reach up, and push my arm out. There was a big crowd gathering at this point, and the next thing I knew, the police had shown up. The officer asked me "Are you stealing mail?" I again said "No. I mailed the letter earlier, and now I'm trying to get it back." He then berated me with questions. "What is your name, where do you live, and where did you get those clothes?" I answered all of his questions, in the order they were asked. Eventually the postmaster showed up in his mail car. The first thing he said to me was "Are you stealing mail?" At this point I was tired of the accusations, but I repeated like a broken record "No, I was trying to get my envelope back that I mailed earlier today." As I was talking to him I looked up, noticed there was a big crowd of people, and lots of flashing lights. Lights from police cars, the ambulance, and blinkers from the taxi cab, and mail truck. It looked like a circus, and I was caught in the middle. I heard one lady yelling in the crowd "What's going on?" Someone replied "The guy in the funny clothes is stealing mail!" Now I was extremely embarrassed, and irritated beyond belief. I yelled back "I'm not stealing mail, Lady!"

    Eventually the postmaster took his key, and opened up the bottom door. One of the ambulance guys reached his arm up, and sprayed me with some weird slippery substance. The other paramedic pulled my arm out the top. It was an overwhelming amount of pain, and my elbow had swelled up like a grapefruit! They wrapped a big ice pack around my arm, and the policeman had informed me "You're coming with me. Come on." The postmaster interrupted him, and said "Wait, there is an envelope with his name on it. Says it was supposed to be sent to Your Father's Mustache in New York." The policeman asked what kind of company that was supposed to be. I explained it to him, about the bars and the bands. The postmaster then proceeded to inform me "You have to come to the post office and fill out some paperwork." I asked him if I could get my envelope back, but he replied "No, once something is mailed, it's the law that it has to be delivered." The policeman then joined in on our conversation "I've got some paperwork for him too, and it starts out with handcuffs. I need to take him to the police station." Well, I went to the post office by way of police car, and filled out the report to the postmaster. On the table was my envelope, and inside was my credit card. I thought to myself, if I can just get that envelope, then I can get a room, food, and maybe a couple stiff drinks. I pleaded with the postmaster to give me the envelope, but again he told me "Absolutely not, once it's mailed it has to be delivered." The police understood though, and they let me go. The cab driver was also there at the post office to make his statement for the police report. As we walked out, he told me he wanted his $3 fare. I reached into my right pocket with my bandaged arm, pulled out $3, and paid the guy.

The most important thing in my mind was to get a hotel room. I walked to several downtown hotels, lugging my suitcases all the way, and dripping water from the ice pack slowly thawing on my elbow. After hours of searching, I finally found a hotel for $7 a night. It was an old, and rundown hotel. As I walked into the lobby it was filled with cigar smoke, and a couple of guys shooting pool. Only having a few dollars, I rented the room just for the night. I walked up the squeaky staircase with my suitcases, and my arm hurt so bad that I barely made it to the room. The room was as old and dusty as the rest of the place, and the bed sagged in the middle. The radiator was whistling like Jiminy Cricket. Although, the view was great. If I opened the window, I could touch the bricks on the building next door.

The next step was to get money. Earlier in the week, I had gotten a job with Ward Dunkirk, who you may remember I worked with several years prior. I explained to him my situation, and he agreed to give me an advance payment that covered the room for a week, and enough money for food. I couldn't believe that just a little over a week ago, I was in New York with one of the best jobs I could ever, and would ever have. But I felt that the kids were most important, so I gave it up to fly to Fargo to be with them, not expecting to be served divorce papers, lose my money, and be forced to live in a dump. On top of that, I'm 25 years old and I got the mumps. You men out there, do you know what the mumps can do to your walk? You can talk the talk, but can you walk the walk?

The next few months of going to court were rough, but at least I had a job playing drums with the jazz trio at the Holiday Inn six nights a week. We were popular enough, and it was a secure job. I was getting back on my feet, taking classes at Moorhead State, my divorce was final, and I finally rented a great apartment, with a swimming pool. No more whistling radiators.

Please Mr. Postman ~ The Marvelettes

It Happened One Night

In 1970 one night while working with Ward, I looked out over the dance floor, and a beautiful woman caught my eye. I searched for her in the crowd, and once I found her, sat down to introduce myself. I told her that I loved the way she danced. She told me it was good music to dance to. Her girlfriend was sitting with her, and she agreed that the music was kicking. I took it as a compliment, since I was with the band. I asked if they had any requests, and she asked if I knew any Beatles. Who doesn't know the Beatles? Ward did know a few, and she requested *I Want to Hold Your Hand.* After we played the song for her, I couldn't take a break for another 45 minutes. I was terrified she would leave, but as luck would have she waited for me. Once our set was finished, I went back over to continue our conversation.

She told me her name was Shirley. Currently she went to Moorhead State University, where she was a freshman. We exchanged information, and from that night forward we embarked on a four year relationship. She was from a small town, about 40 miles from Moorhead. In her family, she had 11 brothers and sisters. When she came to Moorhead for school, it was like a big city experience for her.

The first time she came to my apartment, it was pouring outside. In her hand, she carried an umbrella. I remember thinking that that was so cute. It almost had a romantic quality to it. I watched her walk through the gate, and all I could think was "Man, I can't believe she actually came." We were together day, and night. We spent lots of time at my apartment, which had a swimming pool. I had many good neighbors at that apartment, and we would mingle frequently. That apartment is where Shirley taught me to play chess. We would sit for hours, and hours, and play each other. Sometimes she would miss class because we lost track of time.

I also introduced Shirley to my jazz collection. It was right after I'd purchased my first stereo system. I had an extensive number of records, which I was glad I didn't lose in the divorce. There was one Tony Bennett album, where he sang The Beatles song *Something*. We both loved listening to that arrangement. It was one of the many activities where we could just sit for hours, and enjoy each other's presence. She eventually moved out of her dorm, and into my apartment.

Shirley was very pretty. Her eyes were a deep brown, and her hair silky and black. Her nationality was half Philippine, half German. Again, no meatballs! Shirley was a like burst of fresh air, after my divorce with Cynthia. I felt like a new man. It was like my world had been opened up to a new beginning, and it was wonderful. We talked with each other about everything, but mostly our childhood, likes, and dislikes. Our bond grew stronger as the days went on.

As a boy, I was very interested in Mr. Romano's work as a land developer, especially his strip shopping mall, which was one of the first to be built. I was intrigued at how he had put all those stores together, and it planted the seed for my interest in buildings later on in life. As I traveled around the country with the various bands I worked with, I was always very interested in local architecture, which I documented with my 35 mm camera. I was also interested in trends across the country, and how they affected retail. Such as how New York was far ahead of the rest of the country, and moving into mod fashion. Trends were moving away from the big department stores there, and shifting into small boutiques. Meanwhile, the west coast, especially San Francisco, was stuck firmly in its flower-child phase.

At the nightclubs where I met Shirley, the tables would be filled with all types of people from different walks of life; college students, businessmen, artists, etc. Oftentimes a table would invite over a member of the band for drinks, and conversation.

One night a table called me over, said they enjoyed the music, and started asking me questions. They would ask me things like "Tell me about yourself..." or "How'd you end up playing drums?" I soon picked up on the fact that they were prominent local business owners. One owned a clothing store, another owned a paint store, and the last owned a big department store. All of which were located in downtown Fargo.

I told the department store owner, Michael Herpst was his

name, that I had been all around the country, and seen the trends in his line of work. I talked with the business owners of my recent travels, and of what I had seen related to retail business and the fads of the time. In most cities, malls were being built in the suburbs, leaving downtown areas vacant. A few days later, the businessmen came back into the club, and approached me about my opinion on how to revitalize the downtown area. I shared with them not only my experiences, but my thoughts.

We were focusing on one block that had about four buildings on the west side. I told them that I thought there should be boutiques on the bottom levels of the four building, and they should create interior hallways to go from one building to the next like an indoor mall. I also thought to include a large staircase to the second floor, where there would be a small snack shop and more boutique shops. The timing was just right. Fargo was a big college town, and since Woodstock was still fresh, it was still influencing the styles that the students wore. It was the Hippie generation. I was still wearing bell bottoms, and flowered shirts, so I was three to five years ahead of my time in the Midwest, which doesn't keep up with fashion like the big cities do.

The businessmen took me up on the idea, and the plans were put into action. We filled the stores up within weeks, and the indoor mall was a success. I myself put in a hot dog stand that was influenced by the New York City street vendors. It was called The Dog House. My burst of creativity, I owed to Shirley, my new love. I even wrote a play at the time called *A Song for Nancy*. I also wrote, and filmed several commercials for a local television station, and we got to open a second Dog House in Detroit Lakes, MN, a resort town forty miles away.

On a trip back from Detroit Lakes, we'd fallen off my motor cycle. It was a crash in a sense, because the bike had fallen on its side. Shirley burnt her leg very severely on the muffler. I had to take her to the ER, where she was treated for a 3rd degree burn. To this day, there's still a scar.

Though I was still working with Ward, the business community in town now wanted me to run for Mayor of Fargo. Evidently, they thought I was quite talented at predicting the future in retail. I owe credit to Dominic Romano. When he built that subdivision, and his first shopping center in my neighborhood when I was a child, he became my inspiration.

In 1970 I received a call from my mother Louise, and she said Dominic Romano had passed away. He was born in 1901, and died in 1970. Only 69 years old. I believed that he was murdered in his office by his housekeeper, secretary, and lawyer. The day before his death, a lawyer that Dominic had never worked with before wrote out his will, stating that all his assets would go to Guy, the housekeeper, and his secretary in the event of his death. They would receive a monthly revenue from the water company that Dominic owned, the house, and a few old

Cadillac's. There wasn't much left because of what his legs cost him. Although the will was never signed, the lawyer claimed that it was Dominic's last wishes.

It was rumored that he died from strangulation, and complications of his diabetes. In Guy's statement, he said it was his routine to drop off Dominic in front of the office building every morning, and then go park the car. Dominic, meanwhile, would wheel himself into the elevator, and go to the second floor, where his office was. Guy would then come back to the office to check on him. He said he was walking down the hall to get to Dominic's office that day, when he saw Dominic dead by his desk. The lawyer, and secretary were in his office, both screaming, "Oh my God, Dominic's dead!" Was it murder? The lawyer told Guy he was just stopping by after he'd finished typing out the will for Dominic to sign. By coincidence, the secretary married the attorney. Guy ended up living in one of the apartment buildings that the lawyer owned, and drove one of Dominic's old Cadillac's. Was I getting closer to finding meatballs? Or had I lost my last chance? Watching these events unfold made me feel as though I was solving a mystery.

While living in Fargo with Shirley, we were very happy. I even got my student pilot license! I was on a high, literally! Shirley helped me with my studies. However, Cynthia would not let me see my children. I tried, and tried, and tried to see them. One Christmas Eve I brought presents to Cynthia's parents' house for the kids, and she called the cops on me! I couldn't believe it. It was like my custody papers were monopoly money; they had no real value. Shirley and I decided to sell the hot dog stands, and move to Lake Geneva. I gave Ward my notice, and knew I was gonna miss him, but it was time to move on.

After our move, I took Shirley on a vacation down to Miami Beach. We even went to Joe the Bartender's, and had dinner in the room I'd once worked in. Shirley loved Miami Beach. She would lay out every day, tanning on the beach. It was a joy to me, to have taken her on vacation. It was a well-deserved present for her, and it was the first time she'd ever been out of Minnesota.

While we were there, I received a phone call from the front desk asking "Would you like to have breakfast with Ed McMann, and a tour of Ft. Lauderdale, and cocktails at Pier 66?" I thought, yeah I'd like to do those things! The deal was we would go down in the morning for breakfast, then receive a free trip to Ft. Lauderdale for cocktails at Pier 66. The next morning when we went down for breakfast, we were carted up onto a bus with a dozen other people. They drove us to a warehouse, where we were trapped into watching a scam about a new housing development. Ed McMann was there, on a video being projected for us all to watch. All the people there were conned into signing to buy lots at this new subdivision. I knew we had to get out of there, because no way in Hell I was going to sign that contract. I walked up to the scummy sales man and said "I want a ride back to our hotel. Now." All he said to me was "I'll ask my boss, if you can leave." I was infuriated. "Of course we can leave!" The guy was disappointed, and a little ticked off. But he did end up personally driving us back to our hotel. The biggest loss was all the time that was wasted on that situation.

While living in Lake Geneva, we were aware of a new golf country club that was currently being developed, called Abby Springs. We decided to lease a 300 seat restaurant at the golf club, and operated it for a year. Man that was a lot of work. We served breakfast, lunch, and dinner. The hours were insane. I'd be there from 6 am till 12 o'clock at night. There were many staff members; everything from hostesses, waitresses, and chefs.

One Saturday night the dining room was packed. There was lobster, and steak at every table. That night the chef came up to me, and demanded a raise. He said to me "Vinny I want a raise, or I'm walking out." I told him "Yeah, yeah. We'll talk about it on Monday." He said "No, let's talk about it right now, or I'm walking out." There I was, standing in the restaurant, supervising the going-ons of the place. Steaks were cooking, waitresses continued to take orders, and I had no idea how to man the grill if we lost the chef. I had no choice, I ended up agreeing to pay him an extra $100 a week. He went back to the kitchen, and everything carried on as usual.

The members of the club were mostly from Chicago. One

night the ex-Governor of Illinois, Otto Koerner, came in for dinner. I sat, and chatted with him for about an hour. He was friends with Dominic Romano, and was the Governor at the time when Dominic built his famous development. I thought it an amazing coincidence to be sitting with him now, thirty years later.

Shirley loved the Lake Geneva area, because she had never traveled before so it was all very exciting to her. She met many friends there, and we would go see shows at the Playboy club together. Lake Geneva is a very elegant and beautiful place to be. I'd always dreamed, since military school, that I would build a house in Lake Geneva.

One night at the restaurant, I was approached by a man, who was producing a TV show in Joliet, and was looking for someone to host it. What a coincidence that that was where my parents lived, a hundred miles south of us. I interviewed, and got the job so Shirley and I sold the restaurant, and moved to Joliet. We moved in with my parents. Can you believe that? After all these years, all the houses I'd lived in, the places I'd been, I was back in Joliet living with my parents.

I was the host of a show called *Friends*. It was an hour long cable TV show that aired every Monday through Friday. Cable was just starting to become popular. We were new, and only had about ten thousands subscribers, but they were growing every day. I loved that job. Though the teleprompter was quite difficult for me to read, and I mostly improvised. Regardless, the job was incredible. I would interview guests from all walks of life. I had everyone on my show, from the Mayor, City council members, experts on everything from skiing to cycling, several doctors that gave health advice, and even the Chief of Police. There was even a segment on the show where I'd compare prices from different grocery stores. Our viewers really looked forward to that part of the show. I was even one of the first talk show hosts to do a live remote satellite broadcast.

After about nine months, the station was bought out by the same company that owned Seven Up. My TV director, Woody, left to work for Jimmy Thompson in Springfield. He was the communications director for Governor Thompson, and his job was majorly upgraded. The new owners no longer wanted to do live studio broadcasts, so they obviously no longer needed a TV host. My co-host and I were out of the job. She went on to model. I wasn't sure what direction my life was going in, at that point.

My mother was still a workaholic at her beauty shop. She needed help moving everything in the shop to a new location because after twenty years, the landlord was going to knock down the building. Shirley and I, after being involved with the boutique mall in Fargo a few years earlier, and the building the club house in Lake Geneva, had gained a lot of knowledge on business. We explained to my mother that we should build our own building where she could have her beauty shop that also had rental units for boutique shops. After lots of convincing, she gave the "okay", and we went ahead with it. My mother now had a brand new modern beauty shop, and rental income from all the other shops. There were dress shops, gift shops, and even an art gallery which was targeted towards women.

During the period of building the beauty shop, it was very stressful on Shirley. I had no income, and I was spending all my time, and money on building the beauty shop. Shirley left me and went back to Fargo. My heart was broken beyond belief. We'd been together for four long years. The trauma I'd experienced with Cynthia was of no comparison to when Shirley left. I was lost physically, and emotionally. I moved back to Lake Geneva to a one room apartment, and my friends got me a bar-tending job. I tried to distract myself, but I missed Shirley so much. In talks we had, she didn't want to come back to me. She'd met someone new. I was depressed, and didn't want to live without her. I bought a gun, and decided I no longer had the will to live.

But I wanted to see Shirley one more time. I flew to Fargo, and checked my suitcase with the gun in it. When we landed, I got my suitcase, and hailed down a cab. My thought was that I had to see Shirley, and if she didn't come back to me, I was going to shoot myself. In the cab, I started loading my gun. This was the first gun I'd ever purchased, and I'd only ever seen guns in Westerns before. The driver looked in the rear-view mirror, saw me putting bullets in the gun, and shouted in surprise,

"What are you doing?!" He pulled over immediately, turned around in his seat, and pointed a gun back at me. I couldn't even move. He screamed at me, "Are you trying to rob me?" And I said, "No sir." I told him my story, about how I was going to shoot myself if my girl doesn't come back to me, but I just couldn't get the bullets in the gun. The guy got out of the cab, walked around to where I was, opened the door and said, "Let me help. This is an old gun, the bullets you have don't fit." I said, "Well, I have to have bullets or she'll think I'm not sincere." He helped me load the gun, just shoved the bullets in real hard, and then drove me to my destination. I paid him, and all he said to me was, "Good luck."

    I went to the apartment where I thought Shirley lived, but she wasn't home. Her roommates invited me in, and said they didn't know what time she would be home. I sat down on the couch, pulled the gun out, and put it to my head. I told them, "I am going to shoot myself, I just wanted to see her one more time." Her roommates were terrified, and tried reason with me. I never pointed the gun at any of them, just myself. I sat there for what seemed like a very long time. Eventually one of her roommates said he had to go to work. I told him, "Go but, don't go to the police." The next thing I knew, the police were there. I never should have let him leave. They arrested me for having a weapon, and trying to commit suicide. They told me it's against the law to commit suicide, and took me to jail.

Against the law? What were they gonna do, shoot me? I never did get to see Shirley.

When I went to court, I was sent to the hospital for a 60 day evaluation. If you remember the movie *One Flew over the Cuckoo's Nest,* I was in a room just like that. Full of real nuts. When I arrived, they put me in a lime green jumpsuit. It didn't bother me, but it bothered others. Other patients would look at it and say to me, "Just another two days, just another 30 hours, just another 10 hours." I did not realize that the jumpsuit was temporary, and I would be back in my street clothes soon.

When I first went into the restroom, there was a long row of sinks. I walked to the one on the end, back in the corner. That turned out to be a mistake, because as I was washing my face, this big scary guy cornered me. He was about 250 pounds, giant head, bulging muscles, and he trapped me right in. He was slurring his words, saliva was oozing out of his mouth, and he kept saying, "HOW MANY. HOW MANY. HOW MANY." I didn't know what he was talking about so I just said "Five." He replied, "Five that's good, that's good. There's guys in here only have one, or two, or three, how'd you do it? How'd you do it?" He went on asking if I used a gun, I said no, and he said, "That's good, I got eleven, I got eleven. I'm gonna make it an even dozen before I leave here," and then he said to me, "We are going to be buddies, we are going to be buddies." With that, he turned and walked away. I was shaking so bad I couldn't hold the washcloth.

I had realized later, that he was talking about murder. I later found out that he'd been in this nut house for thirty years already. I had about 59 days to go.

In the Nut House, there was a day-room where residents could go to "mingle". There was a big pool table, in the center of the room. Every day at 10 o'clock the staff members would bring out 16 pool balls, hand out the pool sticks, and then go back behind the safe bars of the office door. Every day a guy would come up to me and say "Go stand in the corner, and watch out." I thought why would I do that? I soon learned why. Many of the patients would grab the balls, and start throwing them at random all over the room. They would laugh, and enjoy it. The balls would hit people all over, and leave welts on their victims. I dodged many a pool ball in my day. I only assumed it was a combination of their medication, and the bright colors of the pool balls, that set them off. After all, Thorazine was the choice drug in the place.

One time, they decided to take us on a bus trip to an apple orchard. On the way there, I noticed a strange pattern among the nuts. Everyone was rocking back and forth. They all sat quietly, minding their own business, but they were all rocking! It was all out of sync, some rocking back while some were rocking forth. It was a sight to see. Like waves crashing down on the shore. Back and forth, back and forth. At the orchard, they released us. It was a beautiful place, set back on a hill. It was very relaxing, until one nut grabbed a bunch of apples, and started throwing them at all of us. It was just like the pool balls! Here goes those welts again. Not only were they throwing them, but they were shoving them in any place they could find. Pockets, shirts, pants, even underwear. Who knows the reason why? Oh wait, I do. It's because they're all nuts! When we got back on the bus, all the apples were falling, and rolling up and down the aisles of the bus. Again I found myself thinking, God I hope nobody I know sees me on this bus.

While I was there, I thought of my childhood. The word 'sanitarium' came to mind. I remembered how that was a scary word when I was a kid, and now there I was, in a sanitarium. One day, while I was there, a news crew came to do a story on the place. I got to talk to one of the reporters and said I used to have a television show, and I was the host. I could tell from the expressions on their faces that they thought I was nuts. Finally my 60 days were up and I had nowhere to go but back to my parents' house. Down and out again.

The Way We Were ~ The Beegees

THE DAY I MET A WAITRESS

My friends back home would take me out for breakfast, and lunch often. One morning at breakfast, I met a cute waitress named Linda. She was short, and had long brown hair. Her last name was Ragusa, and her father happened to be Italian. We hit it off real well. Our conversation ranged from her recent separation from her long term boyfriend, to my disappointment from Shirley leaving me. She was a fan of music and architecture, and I'd showed her some of the houses I was remodeling.

Only one month later, we got married. My best friend Eddy, who introduced us, was the best man. I guess I was crazy, and it was a rebound from Shirley. Her apartment was a couple blocks from my parents' house, and she had the strangest dog. Her name was Mooner. Why was her name Mooner? Well that dog would stand with her head in the corner, and butt facing everyone else. She must've been on Thorazine.

While I was back in Joliet, my friends helped me get started remodeling old houses to make some money. It was actually quite profitable when they sold, and I began to save up money. I saved up enough to purchase a run down, twenty-five room Victorian house. I fixed it up, and that's where we lived.

Soon after we got married, two girls came into the picture. It was wonderful being able to watch them grow up. Linda read to them all the time. They loved Children's books, and as for television, they watched Sesame Street and Mr. Rogers. Bert and Ernie were the shared favorites among our house, and don't forget Kermit! Secretly I was learning while we watched those shows, since I'd never really learned in school.

It was a warm and wholesome family experience that I'd never had before. The popular dolls at the time were the cabbage patch dolls. Of course I have to buy one for both of them, which they loved. The home was built in about 1900, and it was a big house with lots of furniture. In fact the house was so big that the kids could ride their tricycles literally through the house.

Things were going great, although I still thought of Shirley almost every day. But, I had a new life now, and my daughters gave me so much joy. I never was close to my first children, but it really was a lovely feeling being with the younger two. Until I came home one night from work, and Linda told me she was going back to her old boyfriend, and she wanted a divorce. I really didn't see that one coming. We'd been together for four years. The song that comes to mind is *A House is not a Home* by Luther Vandross. I was left alone in our big Victorian. Linda had taken every single piece of furniture. I was sleeping on the floor.

The court battle began over the custody of our daughters. I was granted every other weekend visitations, and some holidays. I was so close to my daughters. I spent $10,000 trying to guarantee my visitation rights. Linda never respected my rights, and I was always taking her to court to have the visitation order enforced. It was an uphill battle, but I never gave up. When I managed to visit, it was always inconsistent. If I showed up to get the girls, she wouldn't let them come out with me. The few times I could spend with them, were lovely.

I sold the Victorian house, and moved back to Lake Geneva once again. I started building a house in the country there. I designed the bedrooms for the girls, so that they could each have their own rooms. Although I was successful remolding houses, it was not my first love. I missed my TV shows, and I missed playing music.

On September 29, 1983, I received a call from WLS-TV channel 7. They wanted me to audition for hosting a daytime noon show. The name of the show was A.M. Chicago. I was one of the runner ups, but the decision was made to hire Oprah Winfrey. She did the show for one year, and then started her own show, *Oprah*. Meanwhile, I continued to work on my inventions, and developing prototypes.

My friend Jack Geoken founded MCI the telephone company, and he offered 50% less for long distance service. I was always fascinated with telephones. I believe being dyslexic had a lot to do with it, because my only form of communication was talking. I couldn't write letters, and cell phones weren't out yet. Although, a few of my friends had car phones, and construction workers had two way radios. Then Illinois bell announces that they're going to charge $.25 for every directory assistance call. This was a concern to me, because I used 411 all the time. I couldn't look up names in the phone book, because I couldn't read the names.

    I invented my new idea in April of 1978. The idea was to offer directory assistance for half price, 12 1/2 cents. Our customers would call in, and before an operator came on the line they would hear a four second ad. The ad would say, for example, "This call has been brought to you in part by Blue Cross Blue Shield." The ads are what generated revenue, in order to discount the call. Then the operator would ask, "How may I help you?" I started trying to work with the phone companies, but of course I was their competitor. I went to meetings in Chicago with Illinois Bell, and Bell Labs in New Jersey. There was a lot of resistance. They did not expect competition from me, just like they didn't expect competition from Jack Geoken, the owner of MCI. My research on the 411 had unveiled some shocking statistics. There were tens of millions of directory assistance calls placed each day. Some companies would have to pay phone bills up to $40,000 a month just in directory assistance calls. I called up some these companies, and told them they should to switch to my system. With my system, they would save 50% on their monthly phone bill. The phone company AT&T had a monopoly on phone books, so they had the name and phone number every customer in the United States. Whenever people moved, the phone company would know their new phone number, but AT&T would not share these numbers with me.

That became a problem because my operators were using phone books I had collected. I collected nearly every phone book in the United States. At one point I had whole rooms full of phone books. But now, the books weren't current anymore, they were only about 70% accurate. The phone company had me in a box. For the next several months the question I had for everyone was, 'who owns your name and phone number? Is it you or the phone company?' They would not share this information with me and their attorneys were rushing to legally stop me.

I continued operating but I was only about 70% accurate, and to beat the competition, I needed the big companies' daily updates. They definitely did not allow any competition. In MCI's legal battle over long distance pricing, they had won their lawsuit against AT&T for having a monopoly. It was federal Judge Harold Green's decision. I wanted the same legal decision for my right to have access to the current directory assistance data base. In the meantime, before the case went to court, I chose Milwaukee, Wisconsin to open my first office. 1984, I formed a Wisconsin corporation called "Milwaukee Information Service," and got a few stock holders. It was about an hour drive from Lake Geneva to Milwaukee. I started working with GTE, WANG computers, IBM, and REXNORD. I was part of a group called the smart group. They were doing local telephone service, and long distance so they invited me to provide the directory assistance. Together we had a complete phone company.

 I was planning on hiring 7,000 operators for the home office in Milwaukee. I figured that would cover all 50 states, 24/7, but soon there would be an unexpected interruption to this venture.

The Java Jive ~ The Ink Spots

SHE WAS SPEAKING GREEK

I left my office in September of 1984, and I met a lady by the name of Elaine. She was short, thin, with glowing green eyes, and classic brown hair. Very cute. She was having dinner across the table from me, with her brother and sister-in-law, and was eating a Greek salad, which is what started my conversation with her. I told her that as a young boy I used to work in a Greek Grocery store. I used to sell Greek olives, and feta cheese to Greek women with Babushkas. We got to talking. As it turns out, she was of Greek ancestry, and spoke the language. As you remember I spoke a little Greek from my earlier years, so we got along well. We hit it off, and decided to plan a date. I know you're thinking, here he goes again with another chick. You're probably right. *Life is like the seasons, first there's laughter, then those tears.*

About three weeks later, on my birthday, we enjoyed dinner at a famous mafia restaurant called Sally's Steak House. Many prominent figures ate at Sally's, including the Mayor, Chief of Police, and head of the mafia. The owner, Sally Papia, was quite a character. On one side, she had the mob in her heart. It was even rumored that she threatened to burn down the restaurant of a man who owed her money. On the other side, she was a very caring and generous person, and an icon in the town. It was a night to remember.

Eventually, I met her family. Her dad was an attorney in Milwaukee, her mother was a housewife, and she had two sisters and one brother. When I met her family, I felt a closeness like I did with Lenny's, the Italian family that had lived next door when I was young. Although they didn't have meatballs, they did cook with garlic, which I figured was getting there. Elaine and I got along very well. I told her about my daughters, who she got to meet during my visitations in Lake Geneva. They bonded very well together. My kids also met Elaine's parents, and they took to them as well. Her parents also visited my mom in Naples, Florida, where they would stay for a few weeks during the Winter season. My mother, Louise, retired in 1985 after forty years in the beauty shop, and purchased a small condo.

The Playboy health club was just across from my new home, and the kids would spend many hours in the swimming pool there, playing with other children. The Playboy club was truly like a city in and of itself. It was on 3,500 acres of land, had two golf courses, two swimming pools, indoor and outdoor, a ski slope and lodge, its own air strip, horseback riding, four hundred hotel rooms, five restaurants, and a 500 seat theater where entertainers would perform. I did several stand-up comedy shows there. The architecture reminded me strongly of Frank Lloyd Wright. Sitting in the rolling hills of Wisconsin, it was a first class place. This was how I wanted my daughters to appreciate the country and nature of life, much like I did as a child at the military school a few miles away.

  Shortly after the club opened, in the mid 70's, the most miraculous thing happened. A maid had been cleaning a room, when she stumbled upon $50,000 in cash. She took it to the police, which I wouldn't have done. Nobody had claimed it, and after a year the cash was split between the Police Department and the Maid. I wish I'd been that maid.

  Elaine and I had to move into my house even though it was still under construction, because the materials were being stolen, and we needed to keep an eye on the place. We loved it there. It was set in the hills, and was my lifelong dream to build a house in Lake Geneva. Falling in love again at the same time was a marvelous feeling. We would commute back and forth to Milwaukee every day. She went to school, and I went to work. By that time, I had one of the first dialed mounted cell phones in my car. It had a long black cord, just like a house phone. Except we didn't have service everywhere, like we do today.

  Every other weekend we would drive the 100 mile trip to Joliet, to pick up my daughters from my ex-wife. Linda would not let me see them on a regular basis. Her and her new husband would try to stop me from seeing my daughters, even though I had a court order for visitation. On one occasion, when I dropped them off, Linda's husband attacked me. He had hit me in the eye with a board, right in front of my children. I was taken away by ambulance, and was hospitalized. To this day I only have 30% vision in my right eye. The police did not charge him with assault. Prior to hitting me in the eye, back before I had sold the Victorian house, he had even shot my front door off with a shot gun. Again, the police did nothing. I found out later that Linda's uncle was a Lieutenant in the Joliet's Police Dept., which is my theory as to why they would not charge him with assault.

When Elaine and I did see the kids, we had a good time, at least. Elaine would teach them the Greek alphabet. It was cute when my daughters and she would recite it together. We were set on enjoying the summer of 1985.

We would drive around the lake, and visit many restaurants. I even took her to see my old military school. It was a change for Elaine, leaving the city to live in the country. We did, however, travel back and forth for Elaine's school, and my work. I had a brand new Mercury Cougar. It was a fine car; black exterior, and gray interior. It even had a telephone. On the side, I inscribed the initials E. C. A. which were Elaine's initials.

Living with her in the country was marvelous. Our house had a wood burning stove. On chilly nights, we would snuggle up in front of it, watching the fire crackle. It was a most romantic setting. On the night stand in our room, we had a clock radio which gave off a heavy glow at night. It would always illuminate her face. I would force myself to stay awake, just so I could watch her sleep. I truly believed that there was a future with her, and my daughters.

I Keep Holding On ~ Simply Red

Terror in the Night

About July 17, 1985, Elaine and I were awakened by a very bright light shining in our windows. Our house was in the country, set back on 40 acres. We'd hung a no trespassing sign at the entrance to the property, along with a rope to keep out intruders. There was no reason anyone, or anything, should've been shining lights through the windows. We were both scared out of our wits. The light moved from window to window. First it was at the front window, then the side window, and quickly it moved to the back. It was blinding. We ran up and down the stairs, trying to find a place to hide. Dashing from room to room, jumping in closets, and running into the bathrooms. We even attempted to hide under the bed. There was no phone in the house, just the one in the car. But it was parked in the driveway outside, and there was no service in this area.

  I gathered up the courage to look out the window, and could see the light was coming from a car spinning around in our driveway. I bolted out the front door, grabbed my ax from the wood pile, jumped into my car, and followed the intruders with the bright lights. It was as if they were trying to lure me out of my house. They were driving down the country back roads, and as I followed I tried to get the number of their license plate to call the police. Tragically I couldn't get a signal on my phone, nor could I read the plate because I was dyslexic. Finally, the car stopped in front of me. I stopped as well, and jumped out of my car gripping the ax. I wanted to find out who the driver was, and why on earth he was terrorizing us in the middle of the night. That was a mistake, as four young men jumped out of the car and came after me. I was only 5'5", and I weighed 140 pounds at the time. Some of the boys were quite bigger than me. It appeared that they were going to beat me up. I threatened them, and told em' to get away or I would hit them with the ax. They circled around me, getting closer, and closer. I felt like I was a gazelle, about to be eaten by a pack of hungry lions. I screamed at them "Who are you? What do you want from me? I want to know your names!" But it was no use, they wouldn't answer me. With the ax in one hand, I bent down and tore off their license plate. I told them very solemnly, "I will find out who you are." I got back in my car, and drove home to see if Elaine was okay. Neither of us managed to sleep after that.

    The next day I went to the police department, and told them about what had happened. I gave them the license plate and when they looked the number up, it came back that the car tag belonged to the fire chief. The police called the fire chief to ask about his cars whereabouts last night. He said he'd loaned it to his son. Apparently, his son had been using his dad's car to go deer shinning in the country. The policeman made arrangements for me to drop off the fire chief's license plate, and the fire chief and I agreed that the boys would never come back to my property, ever again.

  Approximately ten days later, on a Sunday afternoon, a car was parked by our house. Remember we were deep in the country, with no other houses around. There were four or five occupants in the car. I walked up to them and asked, "Can I help you?" The man in the driver's seat replied, "Do you own this property?" I told him I owned a portion of it. He asked me, "Do you ever have trouble around here?" As I said no, I recognized one of the boys in the back seat from the incident ten days earlier. The mood shifted. In a very serious tone, I said to him, "That kid was told never to come to this property again. This is private property." The man very rudely replied, "I am a Walworth County policeman, I can go on any road in the county I want to." I assuredly told him, "Not this road, this is a private road. Get out of here." They left.

  Later on that night, when it was dark out, Elaine and I noticed someone peeking in the windows. I went out the side door, walked around, and saw two uniformed policeman. I asked them what they wanted, and where was their car parked. They told me they parked at the bottom of the hill, and walked up. "Did you tell some people to get off your property earlier today?" They asked.

"Yes I did, officers." I replied coldly.

"Well, they filed a complaint against you. Now do you want to come with us and give us your statement?"

"Yes I can, but I'm driving myself." So I headed down to the station, gave my report, and while I was there, I also let them know what happened ten days earlier. After that, I left and went home. Five days later, another car was parked by our house, with four or five young men in it. I was getting extremely tired of these intrusions. I got the license plate number, called the police, and they said no crime had been committed. No crime? These boys had continually trespassed on my property, and I was ready to take some action. However, the police did say one of the boys, David Ezel, was a convicted burglar in Walworth County. Interesting, since he was one the boys involved with shining the bright light through our windows. The police would not help us.

On Monday July 29, 1985 I drove to Madison, Wisconsin to make a formal complaint with the state, against the Walworth County Sheriff's Department. The special agent that took my report's name was Elizabeth E. Feagles. She took the report, and advised me to get a private attorney. Sometime in mid-August, I received a call from a detective from Walworth County, who wanted to talk to me about the incident with the four boys out on the country road. He told me I could be charged with four counts of attempted murder. Now this was very serious, so we set a date and time to meet and talk about it. I gave him my statement, at the police department, and he said he would get back to me. Within the next thirty days, I was arrested at my house, taken to jail, and charged with endangering safety by conduct regardless of life without mind. There were no meatballs in jail, just bologna. My bail was fifty thousand dollars. I had to put my house up for collateral, and I bonded out about five days later. It was a complete nightmare. I had missed many meetings with the smart group in Milwaukee, and I couldn't tell them where I had been, or why I had missed the meetings.

Thriller ~ Michael Jackson

THE TRIAL

In March of 1986, the trial began. I had a court appointed attorney, because I couldn't afford a private attorney. Looking back, I was so naive about the whole thing. All the good values one learns in childhood can, sometimes, be very disappointing. I didn't understand why I was arrested. To this day, I do not understand the charges. I believed in my heart that at any moment, the district attorney, or the judge would dismiss the charges, and maybe even apologize to me. I felt Elaine and I were the victims. After all, we were the ones being terrorized repeatedly.

Once the jury was picked, and the trial began. Three of the boys were called to the witness stand, and testified on what happened on the night of the incident out on the country road. Their story sounded rehearsed to me. When I testified, I started my story at my house, and what took place there. The prosecutor did not want to hear about that, he just wanted to know what happened in the country. Even my own attorney didn't want to talk about the bright light. It turned out to be my attorney's first criminal trial defending someone. He was just recently chief prosecutor in Walworth county, but had stepped down and found himself a defense attorney. Of course they had my ax as an exhibit to show the jury. I asked my attorney, "Can you bring the light in here that the boys had as evidence? I would like the jury to see how bright the light was." and then added, "Please show a demonstration by turning off all the lights in the court room to show the jury how bright the light was when they flashed it in my house." This was no little flashlight, I knew it would have corroborated with my story. My attorney said, "Well, the boys probably hid or destroyed the light." I frequently asked my attorney why the boys were never charged with trespassing, and disorderly conduct. My attorney said it would look bad for the police, and prosecutor's case while I was on the stand, especially during my bond hearing, I told the court about my childhood. I told them as a child, I went to military school on Lake Geneva. I also told them that I had been in the community for over thirty years. At that moment one of the detectives on the case stood up, and from the back of the courtroom yelled very loudly, "Your honor, we checked with the military school! They have no record that he ever attended!" This was very damaging to my credibility, for this detective was not on the witness stand. He just yelled it out, and the judge did not object, nor did the attorneys. When the jury heard this, the damage was done. I drove to the military school the next day to talk to the principal. He apologized, and said no we couldn't find your file at the time, but we located it very recently, and yes, you did attend the school for a four year period. He wrote a letter explaining that he had misplaced the file and I did attend, but the court never put in for evidence.

      During the trial they also asked me what kind of work I

was doing. I told them, "I have invented a new system for telephones involving directory assistance calls. I formed a Wisconsin corporation, and I have a few stockholders. My office is in downtown Milwaukee." The district attorney stood up, and said to the judge, "We checked with the state and we found no record of the Milwaukee Information Service." I then presented not only old pictures of me in uniform at the school, but also the corporate papers that were filed with the state. Again, the prosecutor and my attorney did not show the jury my credibility. While I was on the stand, I told the court and the jury about my child and early adulthood. I told them my first job was as a paperboy, and I played in the grade school band. I showed them pictures of me marching with the band, and I told them I spent many years as a professional drummer. I showed them pictures of a lot of well-known people, including Jackie Gleason. Just before I joined the band, they worked the white house with President Johnson, and I in my own band, worked for President Nixon in 1970. I brought many pictures of my music career, television show, and gave them all to my lawyer, but the jury never got to see any of them. In addition, I explained to the court that I was studying to be a pilot, and I had my student license. Again, the jury never got to see my license.

  I have to commend the D.A. He was doing a great job on discrediting everything I tried to say or prove about my background. It seemed like nobody would believe me. About a week into the trial, the fourth boy appeared in court, after having been on vacation with his parents for the last month. He took the stand, and told the story of that night. He said yes, they were out shinning for deer, and that they did see me following them out into the country. What he said next was shocking to the court. He told the court that when they stopped the car, and I was parked behind them, the boys had said "Let's count to five, and we'll all jump out at him because it's four of us and one of him." The whole court room gasped. I told myself that finally the truth had come out. The District Attorney immediately called for a recess until the following day.

    I was now anxiously waiting for the charges to be dismissed, but the next day we went back into court. I asked my attorney, "Is the trial going to be dismissed, and are the boys going to be charged with attempted assault?" He said that he was disgusted with the prosecutor, and they had both agreed to continue with the trial, but the boys would not be charged with anything. I said to my attorney, "There is documented proof of the boys coming by my house on two other occasions, let's tell the court about that. Also about the off duty policeman harassing us." My attorney said he would discuss it with the prosecutor. The prosecutor said no, and the jury never got to hear about my complaints. The prosecutor asked the court to have me interviewed by the state psychiatrist. The reason was because earlier I told the court I was dyslexic, and couldn't read. They were using my testimony about playing in a band, working with President Nixon, having a TV show, having an invention in a directory assistance corporation, having stock holders, and having my pilot license, all to discredit my credibility. My bond was revoked and I was put back in jail to wait for this doctor. When I interviewed with the psychiatrist, and he gave me an IQ test. It came back at about 65, which is apparently very, very low. He asked me, did I in fact work with President Nixon? I told him I had, then he asked me,

"You are a pilot?"

"Yes. I have my student pilot license, and have soloed on many occasions."

"Then how would you fly to Australia?"

"I have no idea. I guess you would go south. I don't know, I'm just a student pilot. I fly a small plane just in this area, and it only goes 90 miles per hour." So he just laughed, and diagnosed me as a paranoid schizophrenic with delusions of grandeur. That was exactly what the prosecutor wanted to hear, and now he got to tell the court that my past work could not have been true, because I did not have the intelligence to do that work. He then told them I was paranoid, because I thought people were coming to my house. The prosecutor said my testimony of working with President Nixon was a serious sign of mental illness. The jury believed anything he said.

    Elaine then took the witness stand, and testified about the

night. She called it a home invasion. She also testified that I did indeed have an office, and I had met with stock holders on many occasions. The prosecutor discredited her by asking her, "Do you live with Mr. Herr?"

"Yes."

"Are you married?"

"No, we are engaged."

So again he repeated, "You are not married, but you are living with him?"

"We are engaged to be married." The prosecutor then stated, she must be a biased witness. She told the court "No, I'm just telling you the truth about what happened." The prosecutor ended with, "No further questions."

During the trial I never had any character witnesses, because I never wanted to embarrass any of the stock holders or the smart group. My attorney kept assuring me that we were going to win. It was a long trial that final day. It started about 8 am, and the trial was over by 11 am. We were exhausted, but the judge instructed the jury to go in, and make a decision. It was mostly middle aged and elderly people on the jury, so they were especially exhausted. The jury came back around 1:30 in the morning; the verdict came back *GUILTY* for endangering safety. Approximately two weeks later, the judge sentenced me to three years in the Wisconsin prison system.

There I was, going to prison. After I'd been continuously

harassed for weeks, I was the one going to prison? They placed me in a small cell, and I asked the guard, "Why am I in this unit?" He answered, "The prosecutor wrote a letter about you being mentally ill, and how dangerous you are. You were convicted of a violent crime." After a week, they put me in a larger cell, but the whole thing was still like a bad dream. I kept waiting for someone of authority to let me out. But you see, the state employees, the police, the prosecutor, the judge, the psychiatrist, and the prison system never wanted to step on anyone toes. They all work for the state, and it is not a fair system. My attorney even worked for the state.

However, after a month or so, there were two guards that came and talked to me. They said to me, "You don't belong here, especially with a three years sentence. You should be in the minimum security." One guard even said to me, "You must have really pissed someone off in Walworth County." The inmates where I was were serving hardcore sentences. Most of them had been criminals all their life. These guys were big, burly, scar covered, inked up criminals. Here I was, just a little guy from the suburbs, who'd been falsely convicted. Nothing was ever done to get me transferred.

While in maximum, I had weekly visits with the prison psychologist. We would talk about my case, and my life. I told him stories of my life, and about my accomplishments. I could tell in our conversations, he believed everything I said. He was the first person to believe me. We got along well, and he turned out to be a huge jazz fan. He found I was very well informed about artists of the jazz era. It was something we could share, since not many people contained an extensive knowledge on the subject. It did seem that he didn't want to interfere with the court's decision. "You're just gonna have to grin and bear It." was all he told me.

During this period of time, Elaine went back to her parents' house, because she was too afraid to stay in our house alone. The deed to the house had been put in her name as an engagement present. She wrote me many letters, and it appeared she had a breakdown and lost everything else too. She was invited to go to New York with her girlfriends for a weekend. My mother even gave her the money for the trip. While in New York for the weekend she met a man, a Greek attorney. Within a very short period of time, she had married him and moved permanently to New York. It was devastating to me. It's very hard being locked up in a cell while dyslexic, consequently not being able to write anyone letters, and not being able to make phone calls. I was all alone.

After about one year, I was transferred to a minimum security in Wisconsin. I was a trustee and had work detail, believe it or not, chopping trees with a few others inmates. Could you believe that they gave me an ax to work with? I also worked on a farm feeding cattle. We would spend almost 10 hours a day working on the farm. I tried to make the best of my time there.

I ended up joining the prison jazz band. You wouldn't believe the characters I met. Our band was composed of a bank robber, addicted pharmacist, and some guy who wanted to start his own country, I remember he was always wearing a turban. I'm not quite sure why the last guy was in there. Who knows? They were all incredibly gifted. To think, they could've made a living from their music.

One day the guard came up to me and said I was free to leave. I'd been in minimum for 24 months. I sat down next to a cow, named 411, and had a conversation with him. Then I started crying because the nightmare was finally over. I'd lost everything, again. I believe the hardest thing I've ever been through, was being sent to prison for a crime I didn't commit. I never swung the ax at those boys, no one was hit or hurt. I was simply defending myself, Elaine, and our home. I am bitter, yes, and disappointed. I always believed that people, and that power should be honest and fair. Now I know firsthand that it can be a corrupt system. Shame on all those involved. You may think something like that could never happen to you, especially just defending your own home. Trust me it can.

Hurricane ~ Bob Dylan

THE RELEASE

I was released in April of 1988. They put me on a bus with $60 in my pocket, and dropped me off in downtown Milwaukee. I went, and checked into the local YMCA. There was only enough money for me to afford a few nights. I was lost, lonely, and everything I had was gone. My office, house, car, and dog had all been taken from me. I hadn't seen my kids for almost three years, and Elaine had abandoned me. I wonder how Burt and Ernie are doing.

I was walking the streets like a homeless person. I would go to restaurants that we use to frequent, sit in the same booths, and think of her. I couldn't afford to order, so I would stay until I was asked to leave. I would also go by restaurants, and just hold the doorknob again, in places we used to go. I would go walking in the business district where I once had meetings, with some the biggest companies in the world.

The clothes I was wearing were in shambles. I was wearing the suit and tie that I had been wearing the day of my sentencing, and coincidentally, my last meeting. The suit had been in a box for all those years, so it was terribly wrinkled up. My right wingtip dress shoe had all the stitching worn out in the sole from all the walking I had been doing, so it would flap out under my toes every time I took a step. Not being able to afford a shoe repair, I bought some duct tape and wrapped up the toes. I hadn't shaved for about a week, my fingernails were grown out, and I was walking around in alleys, hoping not to run into the executives I'd once worked with. The busy city life I'd once lived, carried on without me. I was now stuck in the gutter, and time seemed slow. Days dragged on endlessly.

Elaine had put some of our furniture in a storage unit in downtown Milwaukee. I would go there some days to just sit and feel the memories of when we were in the house. I could still smell the house, and the deep scent of the country. Sadly I had no money or place to put the furniture, and the storage unit was many months behind on pay. The furniture was slowly auctioned off, to make up the lost cash that we owed. After about two weeks on the streets, I finally called a friend in Lake Geneva named Herbi. I had bought my property near Lake Geneva from him. I asked him if he could lend me some money. He graciously said yes, and met me in Milwaukee to lend me $900. This was enough for me to get a small apartment, and get what was left of my furniture out of storage. I wasn't surprised when there was no bed left for me to sleep on. As soon as I could, I started looking for a job. I started hanging out at this jazz club, and playing drums two nights a week. That was enough income to keep me going for a while.

In May of 1989, I heard on the news the story of a young foreign exchange student in Milwaukee, who had been sexually assaulted in her apartment. I knew what it was like to be a victim in your own home, so I decided to do a benefit concert for her. I called on jazz musicians in Milwaukee to join me in this benefit. It was held in a beautiful auditorium on the East side. We raised money for a new apartment that she could move into. I never did meet her.

In 1990, I got to host a national television program on PBS titled the *Evolution of Illusion.* It was about magic. I was filmed in front of a green screen, and interviewed professional magicians. By this time, I knew that my directory assistance business was over. I figured the new thing was voicemail, and again, being dyslexic, I thought this was my answer for picking up and leaving messages. No more having to read or write. I decided that I needed money to start my own voicemail company.

One night at the jazz club I was talking to a business man, and he liked my ideas so much that he decided to invest in my new business. He invested $50,000 to purchase this large computer that would be used to handle voicemail. If you think of the home answering machine as one unit, the computer we purchased could handle about 50,000 of those. Today, we don't think of voicemail as a company, we just know it as a service on our phones. Back in the day, I was one of the first to market, and sell voicemail.

I rented an office on the east side of Milwaukee, an area I loved and was very inspired by. It was sort of like a mini Greenwich Village, and it was just a few blocks from Lake

Michigan where I belonged to a sailing yacht club. Not having a car, I would walk or ride my bicycle everywhere. Yes, I did get new shoes. Getting back on my feet after being misdiagnosed by Walworth County with delusions of grandeur, I now formed a corporation called Private Line Communications, Inc., and I even recorded a comedy album called *It's A Funny World*. For my comedy acts, I worked under the name Vinny Romano, which I thought sounded a lot better than Vincent Herr. It was also easier since I was living on the East side, and it was an Italian neighborhood. It was the start of a very good few years.

  In September of 1990, we installed many telephones lines and computers to support the growing number of customers we had. For the next several years, I spent a lot of time going around and educating people on how voicemail could help them. They used to have to call their office, and have their secretary read the pink slip to receive their messages. Remember the pink slip? Now salesmen in the field, or anyone for that matter, could call our company and our computers would give them their messages. I believe we were charging $9 a month for the service, and it was operational 24 hours a day, with no need for a live operator. It was exciting to me that now I could be creative, and look for new applications.

  We had the movie theaters where you could call in and get the show times. We also had the Milwaukee cell phone companies on board, and we did all their voicemail services for their customers. We had real estate's companies too, where interested parties could call in and hear a voicemail description of properties they were interested in. The list goes on and on. Many articles were written about me and my company. There was a cover story in *The Business Journal*, and the magazine was put on every airlines from Milwaukee to New York, targeting not only business customers but all walks of life. There was a picture of me, as the founder of Private Line Communications, Inc., spread all across the country. Other articles in the issue included; The Milwaukee Sentinel, and the UWM Post. We were doing great marketing, and advertising on radio and television shows.

    During that time I had many meetings with Wisconsin Governor Tommy Thompson, where we discussed an application that made it easier for state employees divided by departments to communicate. The Governor himself, as an administrator, could make one announcement that could go to every employee in the state. He loved it, but he couldn't just okay it from me. Because of state laws, it had to go to bid. We developed the first voicemail system for the homework hot-line, a service where parents could call their child's school and get the list of homework assignments. One of my proudest achievements was when I created a system, for the soldiers fighting in the Persian Gulf War Operation Desert Storm, to communicate with their parents, and vice versa. Soldiers could pick up messages from their loved ones, and vice versa. This was perfect because of the different time zones in the world, and also to distract the enemy, so that they couldn't trace a call.

There was an MCI office in Milwaukee that my friend founded years ago, I met with them in his office which was on the 38th floor in the tallest building in Milwaukee. I was finally able to communicate my intellectual ideas to my peers, and they loved it. We partnered with MCI. They would be the long distance carrier to connect with our voice mail company. It was so amazing to me, what a startup company could achieve. I just loved expressing my creative drive and knowing that, in the process, we became a household name. As well, I was doing television commercials with my co-host Lisa Austin for American Express Money Grams. We were representing all the Check Cashing stores in Milwaukee, who used many of our voicemail related services. Our company was doing well.
I was creating applications all the time, and new customers were coming every day.

Sadly after about six years of continuous growth, the phone companies started providing voicemail themselves. They had TV commercials, radio commercials, and full page ads. They took all of our customers from us, and we could no longer survive. Our company crumbled to the ground. It was a David and Goliath situation. We were forced out of business. There were no meatballs to be found there.

Freedom ~ Richie Havens

AT LAST

On June 28, 1996, I walked to a happy hour place in Milwaukee, called Pieces of Eight. It was on Lake Michigan, where you could sit and watch the sailboats go by. It was a warm day, and the patio was crowded. I walked inside, and got in a long line to get my free plate of hors d'oeuvres, when all of sudden some woman reached in front of me and said, "I just need a couple of napkins." I turned to look at her, and man was she beautiful. I wanted to start a conversation, so I said to her, "That was very rude." She simply grabbed her napkins, and walked away. My eyes followed her, and I watched as she went and sat at a table on the patio. Sadly it looked like she had a guy with her.

After about twenty minutes, I decided I was going to walk up to her, and ask if I could buy them a cocktail. When I got to their table, I heard her tell her friend, "Here comes that jerk that said I was rude." I introduced myself, and said my name was Vinny. She told me her name was Peggy, and she was sitting with her girlfriend Eileen. It turns out it wasn't a guy, but a lady with short hair. We got to talking. They both worked at Marquette University, which was about ten blocks away. It was a Friday night and they just wanted go out and relax and have a few cocktails. I thought, WOW! I've got a chance. Her hair was unique, short, frizzy, and dark in color. It suits her. I thought maybe she was Greek or Italian, and boy was she beautiful.

Maybe she had meatballs. Turns out, that was not the case. She was Polish and German, but she did however, give me her phone number. The three of us had a cocktail together, and during that time Peggy left to go to the restroom. I leaned over to her Eileen and asked "Do you think she'd ever go out with me?"

"I doubt it." she replied. After we enjoyed each other's company, they left.

As I watched her leave, I noticed she had a long conservative dress on. I turned to the table next to me and said, "See that girl walking out?" they said yes. I told them, "I'm going to marry that girl one day." Once they were gone, I ran back into the restaurant to the pay phone, and dialed the number she had given me just to see if it was phony. I was glad she had her voicemail on, and it was real. Strangely, after being in the telephone business and having many, many phones, I now found myself without a phone. I called back later that night from another payphone. Peggy answered, and we made a date for the next day.

We met at a coffee shop on the east side, which was very romantic, and we got along well. We went for a long walk on the lake, and I introduced her to some of my friends at the yacht club. As we were walking back up the hill to the coffee shop, she fainted. We were next to a hotel lobby, so I brought her in, sat her down, and then I got ice water for her. It was a very hot, and humid day. To this day, I still don't know if she fainted because of me, or the heat.

Peggy had never been married before, and she didn't have any children. She was from Allegan, Michigan. It was basically right across the lake, but she moved to Milwaukee after graduating high school to help her sister. Her sister, Mary, was nine years older and expecting a first, and only child. A girl she named Lisa. Peggy got a job in the print shop of a big law firm, in 1972 until 1978. Later, she took a job with Marquette University in the financial aid department. Mary was working with the public schools of Milwaukee. Peggy fell in love with the east side of the city, because she was intrigued by all the walks of life that could be found there. The East side was a close knit Italian community. It was the closest I'd ever been to meatballs. Family shops lined the streets. The aromas from the stores, and the scents from the restaurants would travel out to the street, and beg you to come in and try a bite. There was fresh baked bread, and newly sliced meats. Giovanni's, Palermo's, Zaffirro's, Sciortino's, and Gloriosos were all authentic Italian businesses that lined Brady St. She had lived there for over 35 years.

Peggy and her sister would take the train to visit their family at their small farm in Allegan, every holiday. Her parents were a middle class, down to earth family. Her father was of German decent, and her mother was polish. Her Dad raised sheep on their property. I ended up visiting them many times with Peggy. There were no meatballs, though. Just Polish Sausage and Sauerkraut!

    I remember the first time that Peggy showed me her childhood room. I noticed there were many thumbtack holes in the walls, and was curious as to where they came from. "Oh, they're from my Beatles posters that I had growing up." Turns out Peggy was a huge fan of The Beatles, and Paul McCartney was her favorite. She even has every Beatles album. Lining the shelves on the wall, she had the *Nancy Drew* series, and even an autographed copy of *Mary Poppins* from P.L. Travers. Her room felt like a safe place. My room had never felt like that as a child.

    I moved into Peggy's apartment on the east side, not far from my old office, and I thought that neighborhood was the greatest place in the world. We would walk to authentic restaurants, all mom and pop types. Serbian, Italian, Polish, German, Indian, Russian, Mexican, and Irish. All kinds, and all within our neighborhood. I taught Peggy how to sail with members from my club. Now that my girls were older, and had cars, my daughters Candace and Emily were able to visit us. They immediately fell in love with Peggy, and she loved them right back. On several occasions, we all met at my mother's condo in Naples. My mother loved seeing her granddaughters. Still no meatballs, but we were like a family. Shortly after that, in the summer of 1999, Peggy got to meet my first two daughters Tiffany and Teres. We had a reunion with all my family in downtown Chicago, at the Blackstone Hotel on Michigan Ave.

with Cynthia, Tiffany, Teres, Candace, Emily, Peggy and I. It was very emotional for me to have my four daughters together. I have to give credit to Peggy for being so loving and understanding, it was the first time that my four daughters all met each other.

Continually I went back with Peggy and Mary to their parents' house. It was the house that her brother, Billy had lived in. Billy was two years younger than Peggy, and had died in a car crash in 1988. When I arrived at the house, it was a small Cape-Cod-style house on 50 acres of land. It was a beautiful piece of property. There were many trees, and a big ravine that went down a hundred feet. As a result, only about twenty acres of it were tillable. My first impressions was that it reminded me of my home in Lake Geneva. It was quite bittersweet. Whenever I visited, I would walk the property, including going down in the ravine. I did that trip for many years. I'm still very close with her family.

Not only did we visit Peggy's family members, but we also frequently went to Florida to visit my Mother. She was retired by then, but was still a workaholic. Her new job was babysitting for wealthy families, in high rise condo's that overlooked the Gulf of Mexico. One time the condo was so large, when the baby started crying, she couldn't find her. She searched everywhere, walking down hallways, looking in rooms, until eventually the baby cried herself to sleep. Some of my mother's funniest stories came from babysitting.

Peggy and I continued to travel back and forth from Milwaukee, to Naples, to Allegan. I now have a family. But no meatballs.

At Last My Love has Come Along ~ Etta James

THE FIRE

It was on a plane ride to Naples, when I met the most interesting couple. John, and Phyllis Mosele. They had 11 kids, and were from Chicago. John was in construction, and Phyllis was a housewife. He told me many interesting stories about his life. I can recall one about his kid coming home from school with a joint, and John said "That's it!" He went out and bought a 147 foot sailboat, took his kids out of school, and sailed around the world with them. On the boat was all 11 kids, John and Phyllis, a captain, and a tutor for the kids. I thought that was wild.

It turns out that John owned a company called International Star Registry. I'd never heard of such a thing. The concept was that you could literally buy a star, and name it yourself. Their family was very well off., and he was always looking for new ideas.

Somehow John's 147 foot boat sank, in Nova Scotia, while docked. After that he purchased a 50 foot Viking motorboat. He even offered to give me a ride sometime, and I gladly accepted. We went out onto the Gulf many times, where I would sit and watch while his friends fished. It was a luxury boat, and I enjoyed every second I spent on it.

It was May of 98' that John invited me to travel the Midwest loop. The Midwest loop goes all the way from Naples to Chicago. The plan was to ride his boat up from Naples to New

York City, then down the St. Lawrence River, where we would eventually end up in Lake Michigan, and dock in Chicago. There were only three passengers; John, Jerry, and I. We never made it.

Along the way, we made many stops in different port towns. One morning, we set out from Port Colborne, Canada, headed off across Lake Erie. After traveling about 9 miles into the water, the strong smell of smoke filled the air. I was below deck, preparing to shower, when I noticed the smoke. I ran upstairs and told John "I think that there's smoke coming from the engine room." Jerry said he'd go take a look, so he headed below deck. He opened up the engine room door, and giant flames emerged. He quickly closed the hatch, and ran upstairs to tell us the boat was on fire. The first thing John did, was activate the fire suppression system. This would, hopefully, put out the fire in the engine room. It was successful, for about 10 seconds. Then suddenly the flames reignited with a huge boom. Now, the main salon was on fire. Everything was up in flames, the furniture, drapes, everything on the lower level.

We all ran upstairs, and called a distress signal over the radio. John, Jerry, and I threw on our life jackets, and headed to the bow of the boat. We were waiting for someone to pick us up, whether it be the coast guard, or some random sea captain. While waiting, the flames erupted, and swallowed the entirety of the boat. There were loud cracks coming from the inside of the boat. All I had on were summer shorts, and a life preserver. It was at that moment John said to me, with his deep, broken English voice "Vinny, walk down the side of boat and go to my room. I got $2,000 sitting on my dresser, just reach in and grab it." I tried walking with my bare feet, but they were burned by the heat. It was so hot, I could hardly walk. I went back and said to John "I can't walk, it's too hot to walk on."

"Try again." and so I did. The flames were growing by the second, and I had to retreat once again. "I can't do it, my feet are burnt." We all three stood at the bow, waiting.

The flames kept growing, and growing. At one point, they grew so intense, that they were coming right at us. We had no choice, we were forced to jump into the water. Jerry went in first, next was John, and lastly me. When I jumped in, I accidentally jumped on top of John. We struggled for a bit, but Jerry managed to pull me off. The water was freezing, and we couldn't do anything but wait.

Eventually, a pleasure boat came to rescue us. The pulled us on board, and wrapped us in blankets. After that, the Canadian Coast Guard showed up. They took us in their boat back to Port Colborne, where we were put in a room to wait. We were given dry clothes, none of which fit, but we were warming up. A gentleman came into the room, wearing a white Coast Guard uniform with a few medals on it. He asked for our names, and identification. All we could do was tell him our names, since all our I.D.'s had been destroyed in the fire. He said "Well I guess

I'll have to believe you." Then he singled me out, and asked "Are you a Mexican?" I told him "No." He then left the room.

Five minutes later another officer came in. He was wearing the same uniform, but with more medals. He asked us the same questions, and we gave the same answers. He pointed to me and said "Do you speak Spanish?" I told him "No Sir, I don't." He then proceeded to leave the room, the same way the first officer had.

Then a third guy walked in, again in a white uniform, but this time with more medals then you could imagine. He told us "I'm in charge." We told him the same story we'd told the last two officers. He said "Well, I don't know if you're telling the truth about your names. But I can give you each $200, and a pass to rent a car or a plane ticket. This is official Coast Guard Business." As he was walking out of the room, he turned to me and said "Were you born in Mexico." I repeated for the 3rd time "No sir." After he left, I said to John "I think we're locked in here." John said "No way. Why would we be locked in?" So John walked up to the doorknob, and tried to open it. Sure enough, we were locked in. "Why would they lock us up?" John said.

"Well John, think about it. We're in a foreign country with no identification, they think I'm from Mexico, and we just sunk a 50 foot boat with 750 gallons of fuel in their water. I think that's reason enough."

About 10 minutes later, the third guy came back. He handed us some paperwork, and cash to leave with. Jerry was going to fly back to Naples, and John and I were going to drive a rental car back to Chicago. We decided to drive to the airport with Jerry, and have a farewell cocktail. As we walked in, the three of us sat at the bar. The waitress came up to us, and just started shaking her head slowly. She said to us "I just saw you on T.V." After that Jerry got on his plane, and John and I drove back to Chicago. It was a long day.

I went back to Milwaukee, where Peggy was waiting for me. It was so good to be back home with her, after almost losing my life. I couldn't sleep that night, nor the night after that, or after that, or after that. I was beginning to feel fatigued. I tried riding my bike around the neighborhood, but I just didn't have the energy. I decided to make a doctor's appointment. After examining me, he felt that I had PTSD from the boat fire, as well as possible chemical poisoning. The chemical poisoning came from the smoke we breathed in, which contained all the fibers from the fabrics, and the chemicals from the materials of the boat.

I couldn't sleep. I felt that my body, and mind were deteriorating. All night long, I would pace our apartment. There were creaks in the floor, and I could hear every one of them. I tried everything to help me sleep; drinking warm milk, reading, and even taking a hot bath. Nothing seemed to work. One night, I even tried all three at once. After about 8 months, I slowly shifted back to normal. I began to sleep again. It was a long 8 months.

That fall, John had bought a new boat. It was a 44' Sea Ray. He invited me to travel with him down to Naples. I agreed, and one early morning, John, Jim, and I set out from Chicago. This time, we would sail down the Illinois River, to the Mississippi, into the Gulf of Mexico, and around to Naples. We headed off on our journey, not knowing where our travels would take us.

We would travel by day, and dock in marinas at night. I recall docking in St. Louis, and the famous arch was right behind us. The boat was fantastic, with all the amenities you could imagine, but that night nobody could sleep. This was due to the Asian carp, which were flying all over the place. These fish are huge, hard, and slimy. Not only were they jumping on the dock all night, they were jumping into our boat! It was a nightmare.

The next morning we headed off down the Mississippi. It was amazing to be on the same river that many explorers had traveled before my time. It was also quite terrifying to travel the Mississippi. There are currents, and undertows in the river. The biggest thing is the giant barges that travel up and down the river. They are 10 times larger than most other boats on the water, and they won't move for anything.

There were quite a number of yachts headed down to Florida that we would pass daily. John was a maniac at the helm.

He would speed down the waterways, and weave through the boats, creating huge wakes in the river. He was always in a hurry. Every night when we docked at a marina, John would have to call on a mechanic to fix something on the boat. We were always going aground with John as captain. During that trip we lost many props, a shaft, transmission, and even a motor one time. I don't know what's more dangerous; John at the helm, or the flow of the Mississippi. If you ever plan to do this trip here's some advice; take it slow, and enjoy the scenery. Save yourself.

      One time while traveling down the Mississippi, coming into Baton Rouge, the weather was cold, windy, and the current was flowing heavy with white caps. All of the sudden, both our engines cut out. We had no power on the port, or starboard engines, and John could no longer steer the boat. The boat turned, and we started traveling sideways down the river. Out of the corner of my eye, I noticed a huge barge coming up the river. Then on the other side, a huge barge was coming down! We were doomed to be squashed between these two giants of the Mississippi. While we were awaiting our fate, a small boat appeared with a man screaming "Take this line! Take it now!" We tied it up to our boat, and he towed us to safety. The man was from a fuel station for tugboats, not a marina. He saved our lives. Afterwards he said to us "Dock around the back of the station, because we got a big one coming in at 3 am. The wake it creates could flip your boat over." We did not sleep well that night. It was constant waiting for that big boat to flip us. When the boat finally came, it didn't flip us. The next morning John hired a diver to go under the boat, and examine the props. He resurfaced with a two inch cable, which he told us was wrapped around both props. He had to go underwater with a torch to cut them off. Then we were on our way, back down the Mississippi. John was out hundreds of dollars again, and our nerves were shot.

About 10 days later, we had arrived in New Orleans, LA. What a historical town. We spent several days in New Orleans, walking the streets. We ate in some of the finest restaurants. One thing is for sure about John; no matter where you are, if you're with John you eat well. John loved to eat. The food was unbelievable. We ate crawdads, shrimp, and lobster; all fresh, and delivered daily from the fisherman. I couldn't believe the rich culture to be found in New Orleans. We met many people from France, and Africa who spoke French. It hadn't changed at all since 68', when I'd last been there with Your Father's Mustache on Bourbon St.

We left New Orleans early one morning, and entered the Gulf of Mexico. It was a sight to see. We traveled across the pan handle of Florida, about 50 miles off shore, spending a few more nights docking and eating well. One of the last legs of our trip, was to Clearwater for the night, and then non-stop to Naples. We had now completed half of the mid-west loop.

That winter, we would go on short trips to Key West, the

Dry Tortuga's, and locally in the gulf to fish. I'm no fisherman, so I would just lay in the sun and tan all day. John loved his boat, and he was on it every day. He was always inviting friends from his building to go fishing, or just out for lunch on the marina. However, after short trips with John, many declined a second invitation. I think it was for their own safety.

In the spring of 99' John again asked if I would like to join him on a boat trip. He wanted to go back to Chicago by way of the Atlantic Ocean. It was a longer trip then we'd taken last fall, but as John always said "It's an adventure!" I agreed to go, and we set off from Naples. We crossed the straight from Ft. Myers to Cape Canaveral, now entering the Atlantic Ocean. It was the same structure as our last trip; travel by day, dock by night. Of course we also ate well.

It was a safer trip, because the water was much deeper. There was less chance of John going aground. At dawn we would travel 50 miles off shore, travel our daily 250 miles, and then head back inland at dusk to dock. We stopped at many towns along the way, where we walked the streets, and ate in restaurants. We visited many southern historical districts along the way.

We worked our way up the East Coast, where we finally entered New York June 6, 1999. It was a clear day, but very choppy. The waterway was filled all sorts of boats, and John said to me "Vinny, take the Helm. I have to go down to the head." It was surreal. I found myself dodging tour boats, sail boats, speed boats, all kinds of boats! There I was again, in the same waterway as the tens of thousands of immigrants who had once come from Europe. Straight ahead was Manhattan, and to the left was the Statue of Liberty and Ellis Island. I could see the twin towers, standing tall above the surrounding skyscrapers. Eventually, John came back up and resumed his position as captain. I was relieved, because John was a good navigator, when he wanted to be. This was the time when I wanted him to be. I could now walk out on the bow, and look at the city from the Hudson River.

That night we docked on the Jersey side of the Hudson, with beautiful views of Manhattan. We ate delicious food as usual, at the restaurants nearby. I hopped in a cab afterwards, and visited my old apartment in Greenwich Village. It'd been 30 years since I lived and worked in the Village. Believe it or not, nothing has really changed.

A few days later, we headed north on the Hudson on our way to Albany, then to Canada across Lake Ontario, through Port Colborne, and down into Lake Erie. Luckily for us, this time there was no fire. We traveled our way back to Lake Michigan, and into Chicago.

John was the most unique man I've ever met. He broke the mold. Never will there ever be a man like John Mosele. He was kind, generous, smart, tough, and most of all the most reckless man I've ever met.

    I sincerely want to thank you John for the opportunity to cruise with you, and for all the adventures along the way. Most people aren't given such an opportunity in their lifetime, and I was lucky enough to do the trip more than once. It is something that I will never forget, and will carry with me for the rest of my life. John, you were like a brother to me. After spending hundreds of hours with you, we became the best of friends. You, your wife Phyllis, and your children have all become an extended family of mine and Peggy's, and will always be.

Love you Brother, Rest in Peace

Light My Fire ~ Jose Feliciano

Always and Forever

As time went on, Peggy and I remained in our relationship. It'd been almost 7 years, and we were still going strong. Many years ago when I first met Peggy, I knew I was going to marry her. On June 29, 2004 it happened. Peggy had given her notice the University, after 18 years of working there. We got married in front of the Justice of the Peace, by a well-respected Italian judge, Honorable Judge John Sanfilippo. Those who stood for our wedding were old friends that I'd met through Peggy's sister. It was a very beautiful ceremony, and we had tears in our eyes. That same day, we moved back to Allegan, taking my mother with us. Her health was failing, and Peggy took very good care of her for the next few years until she had to go a nursing home in Joliet, where she passed away in 2007.

Peggy and I had both lost family members in the early 2000s. Peggy's sister Mary passed away from pancreatic cancer in 2003, and later the same year, her father Bill passed away. We were at both their sides.

We continued to live in Michigan, and from the first day I saw the property her parents owned, I always had in my mind it would be a perfect place for a small country inn. So Peggy and I designed and built an inn there to look like an old barn, which fit perfectly in this community. We built patios off the rear, with views facing wild life and sunsets. We opened in June of 2011.

During the opening, Peggy's mom, Leona's, health started failing. We were forced to put her in a nursing home about a mile away. Peggy would visit her mom every day, sometimes twice a day. Leona eventually passed away in February of 2013.

My brother Sam is alive, and well. Sadly we don't talk much. In his lifetime, he married his longtime girlfriend. They eventually divorced, never having had children. I've never had the experience of being an Uncle.

We are now starting our 7th year working at Hotel Allegan "The Inn Place." Although we are not a bed and breakfast, we are similar. Our guests have been most interesting, and rewarding. They come from places like Chicago, Indiana, and Ohio to attend family reunions, and Weddings at the Silo Hall here in Allegan. Our location is amazing, at just twenty minutes from Lake Michigan, thirty minutes from Kalamazoo, and forty five minutes from Grand Rapids. We are in the country, just one mile from the river town called Allegan. Our guests have been very nice, and love the country setting. We spend the winter months in Naples, where we sailed on the gulf in our sailboat *The Peggy Ann,* and the summer months running Hotel Allegan.

In March of 2017, we had another family reunion with my daughters in Naples. The weather was warm, and we had a great time. The girls stayed in a beautiful hotel, a few miles from our condo. It had a huge pool, and overlooked the Gordon River. While there, Emily called up my cousin Mike, who happens to have a very nice boat, and we all went for a long ride around Naples. My girls loved looking at all the beautiful homes, and staying out in the sun all day. We even took a ride down to Key Waden Island, where there were hundreds of boats anchored. It's all a big party. Reunions are always bittersweet. I got to see my daughters, all grown up and successful. But after it's over, we all have to leave and go back to our normal lives.

Today Tiffani is 52, remarried to a nice guy, and has two children. Her kids are Gabrielle, and Andre and they are in their late 20's. Tiffani, her husband, and Andre live in Phoenix. She sells imaging equipment to hospitals. Gabrielle lives in L.A. where she works in the high end fashion industry. Andre has part ownership in a recording studio, which he loves.

Teres is 50, divorced, and also has two children. She has a son Jonah, and daughter Allie. Teres sells pharmaceutical supplies, which requires her to travel a lot. She is certainly a free spirit. Jonah is a very talented golfer, and he plays all the tournaments he can. Allie travels between Phoenix and Hawaii. She loves nature, swimming, diving, and waterfalls. She often visits her Dad, Jim. Teres lives in Phoenix along with Tiffani.

Candace is 41, married, and has two little boys. Their family lives in Texas. Emily is 39, and lives in Chicago, and works for the Chicago public schools system. She has no children, but is married to a gentleman who owns an art gallery. I'm not sure about Bert and Ernie. All my girls are educated and healthy. I wish we lived closer to each other. But we all have our own lives to live.

My life with Peggy has been the best. Through all the ups and downs we've experienced together, it has only brought us closer. Especially since we've been there for each other through the losses of so many family members. We spend our summer's together working at our Hotel, and the winters in Naples at our condo. Peggy loves Naples. All the stores in our neighborhood, and our beloved condo. She walks everywhere. I, however, like to drive my mustang convertible. We have the perfect balance.

Recently I had my DNA tested, in order to find where I truly belong. This is something I've been pondering throughout my entire life. After all those interesting meetings with Mr. Romano, and the feelings I'd have about my home life. Finally my results have come back, and I can finally understand. Will I find meatballs?

Day by Day ~ The Four Freshman

The Truth Comes Out

My whole life, I've always wondered where I truly belonged. I've always felt like an orphan, even though I had a family. My time was always spent chasing after meatballs, and running away from sauerkraut. All the rumors in my neighborhood, and the suspicions that my Dad was not my real father, followed me around where ever I went. Even though he was always good to me, I was always uncomfortable. I just never felt right living in that house, and felt deprived of my true heritage. The name Herr never fit. After all, Vinny is Italian! When I was at home, with the sauerkraut, I always felt like I was in the wrong place. But when I went to Lenny's house for meatballs, or while living in Milwaukee surrounded by the Italian community, it always felt like I was home.

When I was born, there were no paternity tests to determine who the real father was. But in those days, there was never any doubt who the parents were. There was no need to doubt. DNA, or deoxyribonucleic acid, is a fascinating component of the human body. One little strand can tell you more about yourself than you already know. Where you came from, who your ancestors are, even current relatives you may not know about. In my case, I found out where I truly belong. My DNA, as I'd always felt, was majority Italian and Greek. To be exact, 49%. The other half was Scandinavian, and Eastern

European, from my mother's side. This was something I'd always known was inside me, and now I could have it confirmed.

Recently, results came back with matches of current relatives. I was amazed to find I had cousins, right down the street from where I'd grown up! My real, blood relative cousins. I had the amazing opportunity to contact my 2nd cousin, Karen Lavazza, and learned that she was directly related to Dominic Romano. All my life I'd wondered about the relationship that me and Dominic had had. Now after 71 years, the truth has finally come out.

You might be wondering, how do I feel about this? Well, honestly I feel cheated. My Aunts, Uncles, and Cousins on the Herr side were not really my cousins. I missed out on my real life. My real father never got to raise me, and he died before I knew. I never got to know my Aunts, Uncles, or Cousins on the Romano side. What would my life had been like, if I'd been raised by Dominic? I can only fantasize about the answer to that question. Did I get my learning disability from Dominick? My diabetes? My dyslexia? Was the cause of all my pain, and creativity, attributed from him? I will never know. In this moment, I've never felt so alone. I'm just as lonely as I was as a child.

It's the Dominic affect. My kids now carry all of Dominic's DNA inside of them. They were raised with the name Herr, and that affected them. Their looks never matched their name. My first two, Tiffany and Teres, are Lebanese and Italian. Their olive colored skin, and dark hair reflect that. It's the same with Candace and Emily. I feel like my whole family has been cheated. I am a Romano, my kids are Romano's, and their kids are Romano's. Just recently I found out the names of Dominic's siblings who I never met: John, Rose, Congetto, William, Joseph. I wonder if they knew about me.

After all this time, the pain is still there. Part of me feels like it always will be. I can never go back and relive the lost time. I can only look back at the opportunities that were missed, and the life I always wished I had.

It's been said that you are what you are before you were born. Your mother and father, even before they met, had you inside of them. Their genes, cultures, and emotions all have an influence on who you will be even though you, ultimately, will have your own personality.

My personal belief is that your heritage is important. Where you come from, whose blood runs through your veins, and what traits have been passed down to you. Da Vinci, Galileo, and Michelangelo are all famous Italians who made landmark achievements in this world. The arts in Italy are well known for their opera, architecture, and art. I even discovered that my Grandfather was from Italy, in a little town called Roseto Valfortore. I'm proud to be Italian.

On September 7, 2017 I met with Honorable Judge Michael Buck of Allegan Michigan Circuit Court to request that my name be changed to Romano. He granted my request. He was also impressed with the book I just wrote about DNA testing and dysfunctional families, and ordered a copy. I will now have my real name after 72 years. Thank you Judge Buck.

Who am I? Where did I come from? After all these years the truth has come out. What I've been searching for all my life, I've finally found. It's been there all along, a BIG plate of meatballs.

The End

Shocking new chapter
Letter in the mail
It's a boy!

DNA 50 years later -
But first a very intriguing phone call

A man named Danny Fry called me and said he did an Ancestry DNA test and asked if I was related to any Fry's, for it showed that we are cousins. It sounded like a con to me. Who is this man? Is he for real? I got thinking, yes, my mother's mother who lived in Kentucky had the last name of Fry. He then mentioned some other things that sounded fishy. He asked me if I knew who Colonel Joshua Fry was, for we are related. I said I never heard of him, who is he? He said you can look him up on the Internet but let me tell you a little about him. He was born in England in the 1700's, came to the United States and went to William and Mary College. He was a surveyor, cartographer, soldier and politician best known as the creator, along with Peter Jefferson, of the Fry-Jefferson map of Virginia. He was running for a high office, but tragedy struck and he fell off his horse, hit his head on a rock and died in 1754. An attendant of his funeral was George Washington, who was a friend of his. For more in-depth history of Virginia look up Colonel Joshua Fry on the Internet.

Now back to the shocking letter in the mail. On November 6, 2018, I received a letter from a man named Gene Krumenacher who said he was born in June of 1968. He lives with his wife and 2 daughters in North Carolina. His adoptive parents told him he was adopted at birth and about 2 years ago after 50 years of not knowing who his biological parents were, he decided to do a DNA test to see if he could find them.
He was able to find his mother and he got in touch with her. I personally am not aware of her ethnic background or family. She gave him the name of his father (me) and said I knew nothing about the pregnancy. She told him I was a good-looking man who drove a sports car.

Gene stated that he went to social media, Facebook etc. and found me and the book I wrote, "A House Without

Meatballs." He ordered the book from Amazon which gave him a wealth of information about me and the family. He found out he had 4 sisters, an uncle, nieces and nephews and many other relatives that of course he never knew about. And just think, I found out I had a son and 2 granddaughters I never knew about! Gene contacted his sisters (my daughters). They all decided to meet in Chicago for the first time: Tiffani, Teres, Candace, Emily and Gene. I was not aware of their plans to get together. Imagine 50 years and finally meeting his sisters, and they meeting a brother they never knew of! They were all very excited and got along marvelously well. They keep in close contact and get together as often as they can. In the pictures they sent me they all look alike: Dark skin, dark hair, brown eyes. My first born, Tiffani and Teres, are Lebanese, Greek and Italian. Candace and Emily are Italian and Greek, Gene resembles me and my father (his grandfather) Dominic Romano. In addition
, they all have some English from my mother's side of the family, the Fry's.

I want to mention that we all grew up with the wrong last

name. My four daughters and I all went by the last name of Herr, which was my mother's husband's name. My actual father was Dominic Romano and I should have had that name all of my life, as well as my children. My children and myself were all raised with a German last name, which is so misleading when you look at our features. I truly believe that if we all would have had the Romano name our lives would have been different. For names and cultures and DNA are most important in life. A name represents the original country you are from, the culture, the food, the style hidden deep inside of us. Living life with the wrong name is torment. When women marry, they usually take the man's last name which is accepted in our culture. I believe they should keep their last name by birth as well as the husband's last name, which some do. I'm sure thousands of people have been affected by this.

Let's look at Gene, his wife and daughters with the name of Krumenacher. Would their lives have been different with the Romano name through school, work, social activities? Do they physically resemble German or Italian heritage? What a can of worms. Gene's last name should have been Romano, in respect to me, my father my grandfather and other relatives who were born in Italy. In addition, my grandmother was born in the Mediterranean area of Greece. The name Krumenacher is German, which is Central Europe, a totally different culture. I can testify that going through life with the German last name of Herr has affected me. You see, my characteristics are I am short, black hair and brown eyes. I resemble my father, aunts and uncles on the Romano side. Through my life on hundreds of occasions people have asked me if I'm Italian or Greek and where the name Herr came from especially when I attend their ethnic festivals. These are people that have strong backgrounds of Italian or Greek. Therefore, I know first-hand what's in a name. Also, my first two daughters who were raised in Fargo North Dakota, Norwegian territory, were always asked where the name Herr came from, especially because of their dark features. So, it is my total belief that your true last name is most important.

  Many times, I've been asked the question, how do I feel about having a fifty some year old son I never knew about? If I were to say I feel cheated, that word doesn't even come close. I've been robbed. So has my son Gene and his sisters. I never got to see him as a child. Didn't walk him to school, celebrate birthdays or holidays, never got to play catch with him or see him ride a bike for the first time. Never got to nurse him when he was sick with childhood fevers (remember that red cough syrup?) or dress him on winter days before going outside to play. And what about childhood photographs, from a baby to adulthood, those precious pictures we all look through. I never got the chance to see him grow. So, the answer to the question is yes, I've been robbed. And my heart goes out to all the other parents and children that have been separated throughout their lives. If I would have known I had a son I would have been at the hospital from the moment he was born and would have stopped anyone from trying to take him away from me. I would have taken him home where he belonged. In a quote from Gene's letter to me, he wrote, "We have so much in common as I also grew up in a house without meatballs."

In case you're wondering if Gene and I ever met, the answer is yes. We met for the first time after fifty some years in November of 2023 at a family gathering in Scottsdale, Arizona, five years after his letter to me. We only spoke briefly, but I hope to have more conversations with him in the future.

Finally, all of my children together, the Romanos! (See last photograph of Gene with his sisters.) They are all very close, communicating on social media every day.

Dominic would be proud.

As stated on page 1, "It's been said that you are what you are before you're even born, your mother and father, even before they met, had you inside of them. Their genes, culture, and emotions all have an influence on who you will be, even though you, ultimately, will have your own personality."

Vincent William Romano

Gene with his sisters

"Smile, though your heart is aching."

Charlie Chaplin

INDEX

Woody Allen; Born December 1, 1935, Woody Allen has worked as an actor, director, comedian, playwright, musician, and writer. Allen is from the Bronx, New York. He has starred in 65 movies, and written many plays.
~53, 54, 55, 60

Herb Alpert; Born March 31, 1935, Herb Alpert is an American musician who founded Herb Alpert and the Tijuana Brass. Herb was also a founder of A&M records. He has also dabbled in art during his time. In total Herb Alpert has produced 28 albums total, including 5 No. 1s.
~38, 49

Orson Bean; Born July 22, 1928, Orson Bean is an American actor from Burlington, Vermont. He has appeared on many game shows during his time, and was a long time panelist on *To Tell The Truth* during the 60's and 70's.
~60

John Beck; Born January 28, 1943, John Beck is an American actor from Joliet, Illinois. Beck was also quite the boxer in his day, wining many amateur titles.
~54

Pat Boone; Born June 1, 1934, Pat Boone is an American singer, actor, writer, TV personality, and composer. Boone has been active in the business since 1954.
~58, 59, 164

Walter Brennan; Born July 25, 1894 in Lynn, Massachusetts. Walter Brennan is an American actor who has starred in 230 films. He was in the film industry from 1925-1974. He released 3 albums during his career. Walter passed away September 21, 1974.

~60

Diahann Carroll; Born July 17, 1935, Diahann Carroll was born and raised in New York. She is an American singer and actress. Carroll earned her big break by winning continuously on the program *Chance of a Lifetime*. She is well known for her roles on *Julia* in the early 70's, and more recently *Grey's Anatomy*

~53

Jim Garrison; Born November 20, 1921, Jim Garrison was a well-known DA. He served as DA of Orleans Parish from 1961-1973. Jim passed away on October 21, 1992.

~44

Dave Garroway; July 13, 1913, Dave Garroway was an American TV personality. He was active from 1938-1982, and has a star on the Hollywood walk of fame. He was also the founding anchor of the Today Show. Dave passed away on July 21, 1982.

~59

Jack Geoken; Founder of MCI, which led the way in transforming the telephone industry.

~87, 88

Jackie Gleason; Born February 27, 1916, Jackie Gleason was an American comedian, actor, writer, and musician. He was active from 1941-1986, during which time he starred in countless television shows, and movies. Jackie passed away on June 24, 1987.
~49, 51, 56, 103

Banu Gibson; Born October 24, 1947 in Dayton, Ohio. Banu Gibson has spent her whole life on stage. She trained with dance, and vocals growing up. Banu has also played with many bands in her time.
~51, 61

Paul Hornung; Born December 23, 1935 in Louisville, Kentucky. Paul Hornung was the first pick in the 57' draft by the Green Bay Packers. He is now known as "The Golden Boy" in the pro football hall of fame.
~44

Otto Koerner; Born August 15, 1908 in Chicago Illinois. Otto Koerner was the 33rd governor of Illinois, appointed by Lyndon B Johnson. He served in office from April 22 1968-July 22, 1974. Otto passed away May 9, 1976.
~1, 78

Byron Nelson; Born February 4, 1912 in Waxahachie, Texas. Byron Nelson was an American pro golfer. He was active between 1935-1946, during which he won 11 consecutive tournaments and 18 total tournaments in 1945. Byron was inducted into the World Golf Hall of Fame in 1974. He passed away September 26, 2006.
~60

Jesse Owens; Born September 12, 1913 in Oakville, Alabama. Jesse Owens is an American track star who won 4 gold medals at the 1936 Olympics in Berlin. Owens made landmark achievements. Jesse passed away on March 31, 1980.
~*60, 163*

Dominic Romano; 1901-1970. Dominic Romano accomplished many things in his life. He made history with the building of the subdivision which he named Lidice. Throughout his career Dominic worked in many fields including owning a radio station, movie theater, water company, and strip mall. He even wrote a book. Dominic's list of accomplishments is long and profound.
~*1, 3, 43, 44, 74, 75, 78, 138*

Soupy Sales; Born January 8, 1926, under the name Milton Supman. Soupy sales was an American actor, comedian, and TV personality. He was active from 1949-2009, during which time he appeared on many game shows, and even his own show *Lunch with Soupy.* Soupy passed away October 22, 2009.
~*50, 55*

Chris Schenkel; Born August 21, 1923 in Bippus, Indiana. Chris Schenkel was an American sports caster. He was active for five decades, during which he did numerous sports and radio shows. Chris passed away September 11, 2005.
~*60*

Bobby Vee; Born April 30, 1943 in Fargo, North Dakota. Bobby Vee spent his days as an American singer and songwriter. He was made famous on the day the music died, and he remained active from 1959-2014. Bobby passed away October 24, 2016.
~42

Ed Wynn; Born November 9, 1886 in Philadelphia, Pennsylvania. Ed Wynn was an American actor, and comedian. He played many roles in movies, both live action and voices. Ed also was in several Broadway musicals. Ed passed away June 19, 1966.
~60

Where Dominic read his speech 'Lest We Forget'
Dominic pictured center

Dad holding me as a baby

Wasn't I cute?

My Mother
Louise May Wooden Herr

My childhood home

Dancing up above; 2nd from the left, marching down below middle

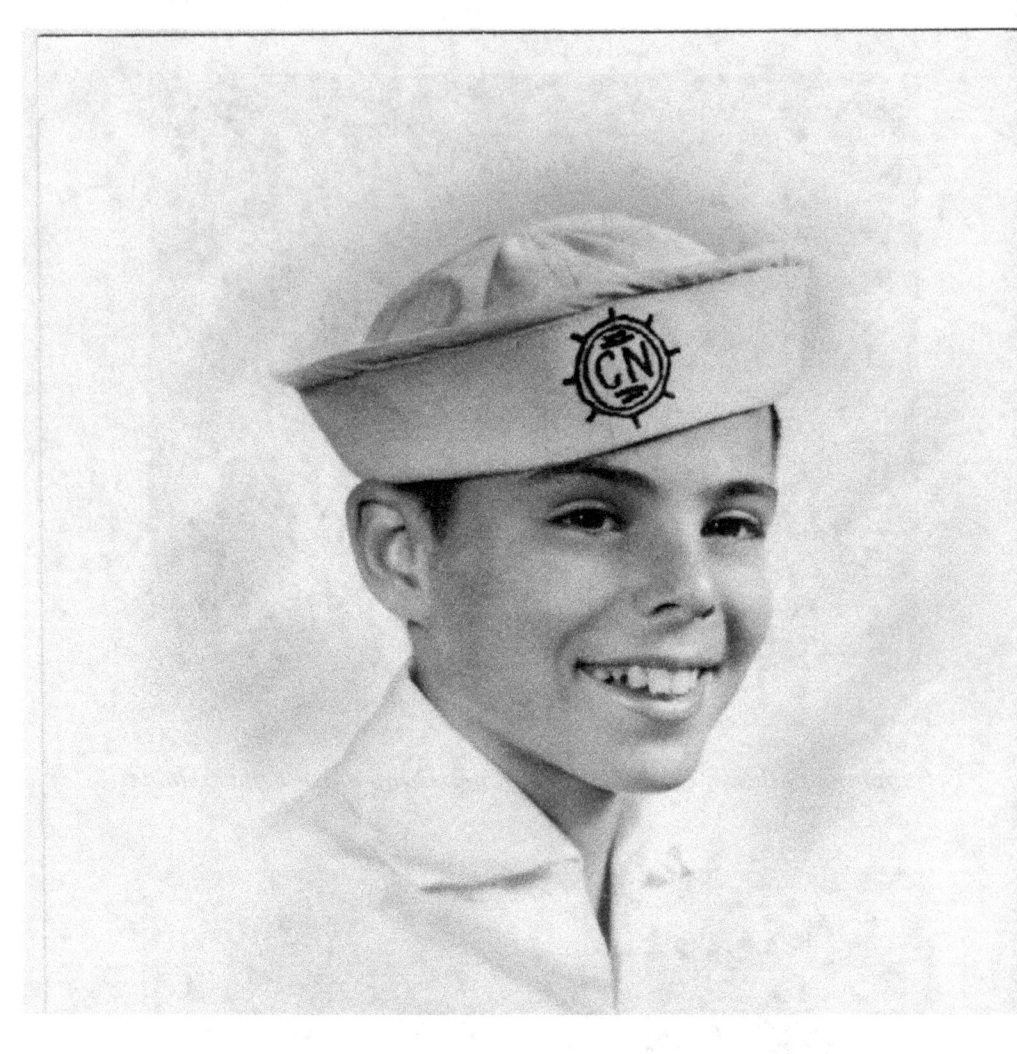

My Military School portrait

My Mother and I taking photographs of each other simultaneously

Our military group portrait. Can you find me? Third row up, third kid from the left

Mom and I on the docks of the Military Academy in Lake Geneva

Me with the schools Christ Craft on Lake Geneva

The Chicago 5 in Fish Creek, WI

My first car, a 1953 Chevy Convertible

Our Show Group

Duane's plane that got shot down. He's the 3rd over in the first row

Cynthia and I

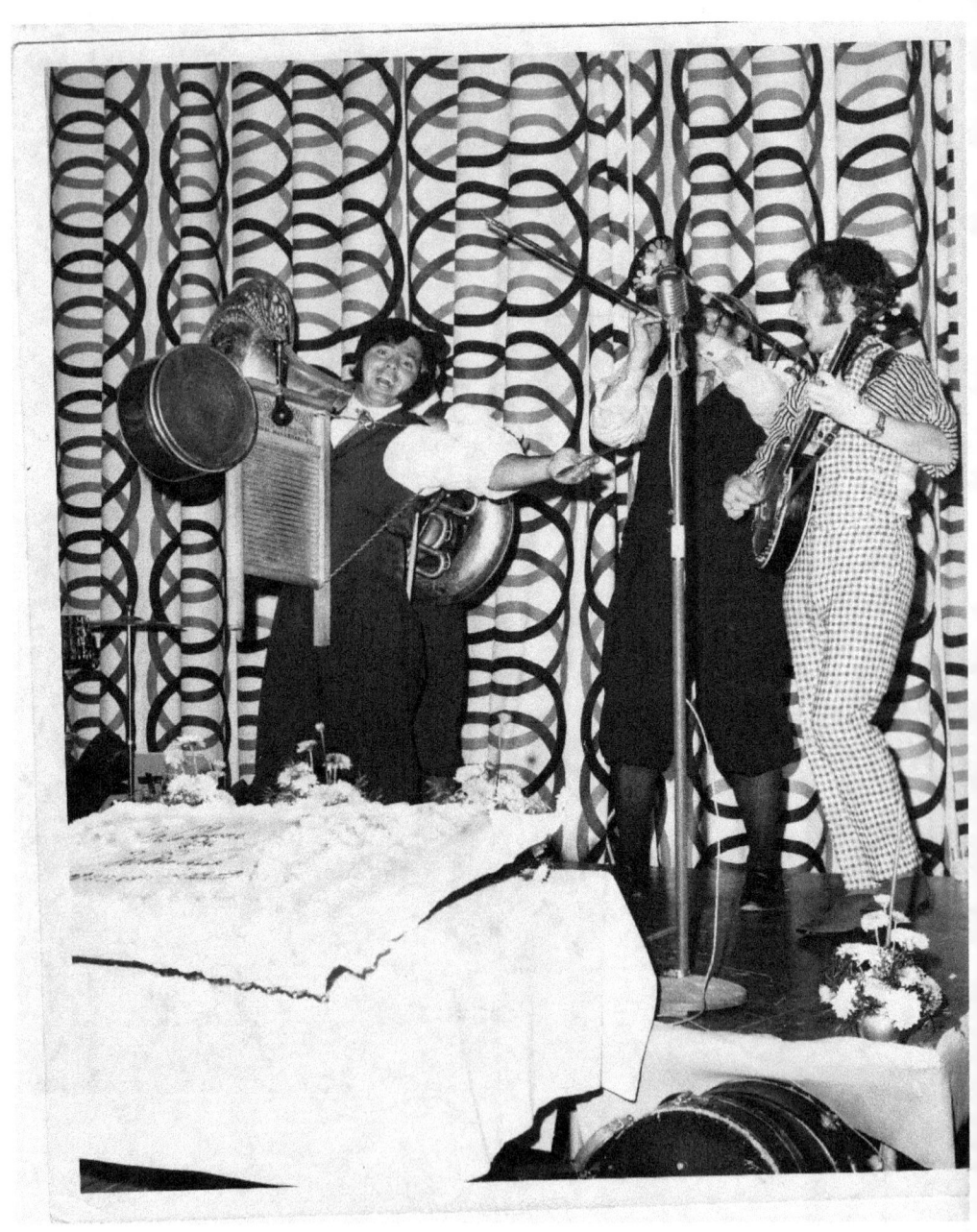

There I Am! The washboard player

That crazy WWI Vet

What a classy looking group! Your Father's Mustache 68'

Jesse Owens and I

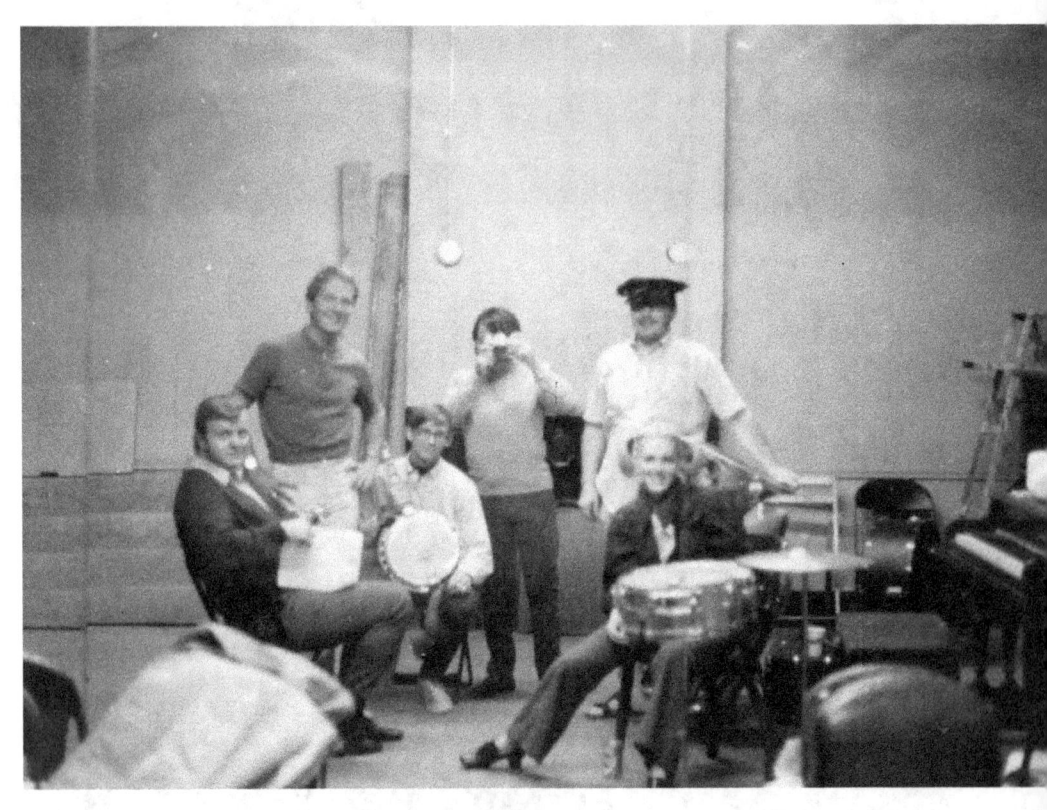

The world's first selfie. There I am taking it, with Pat Boone!

Teres and Tiffani

The Dog House hot dog stand I owned

Shirley in Lake Geneva

My apartment with the pool

Shirley and I at my apartment

My Co-Host Nancy and I on our show Friends

Linda and Vincent's wedding, June 14, 1976

Our Victorian we lived in

Visitation with the girls at Lake Geneva

Christmas at Grandma's house

Elaine

The House I built for my Children

State of Wisconsin
OFFICE OF THE SECRETARY OF STATE
MADISON, WISCONSIN

Douglas La Follette
SECRETARY OF STATE

June 30, 1987

Dear Mr. Herr,

    Regretably the statutes require a minimum fee of $2.00 regarding written requests of copies of corporate documents or information.
    Articles of incorporation for Milwaukee Information Service, Inc. were filed on December 3, 1984. There are no annual reports filed for this corporation putting it in bad standing. Enclosed is a reinstatement report, when filed, will put this corporation back into good standing. If you have any questions, please feel free to contact us at (608) 266-3590.
    Also enclosed are copies of the articles of incorporation which is all we have on file.
Thank you.

CORPORATION DIVISION — Office of the Secretary of State
P. O. Box 7846, Madison, Wisconsin 53707   (608) 266-3590

Proof that I filed corporate papers for my company

COMPLAINT FORM
DJ-DCI-1 (Rev. 9/84)

1. Case Number WP-0-65	2. Date 07-31-85	3. Nature of Complaint Police Harassment

4. Complaint Received (Date – Time)

July 29, 1985 - 10:00 a.m.

5. [X] in p
   [ ] mai
   [ ] tele

7. Investigation Requested By/Information Received From (Include Title)

Vincent W. Herr

8. Address

Box 1059, Brierwood Subdivision, Lake Geneva,

11. Case Title

VINCENT HERR

13. Address

Box 1059, Brierwood Subdivision, Lake Geneva,

15. Facts of Complaint

On Monday, July 29, 1985, VINCENT W. HERR,
the Madison DCI Office with a complaint abo
Deputies trespassing on his property, at wha
hour, and peering in the windows. S/A Eliz
following information from HERR:

HERR is currently the sole resident of the n
of Lake Geneva. He does not have phone serv
under construction. HERR lives at this addres

Partial image of a document I filed as a complaint against the police of Walworth County

Jazz benefit for East Side woman

Drummer Vincent Herr and local jazz musicians will play benefit concerts at 7 and 9 p.m. Friday for a Milwaukee woman who was seriously injured earlier this month in a sexual assault. The benefit concerts will be at the Clavis Theater in the Prospect Mall, 2239 N. Prospect Ave. Admission is $5 per show. Proceeds will be donated to the Friends of East Side Victim account, First Wisconsin Bank, 2303 N. Farwell Ave., Milwaukee, Wis. 53211.

The Jazz Benefit I organized

Education
Homework hot lines help parents keep kids on track

By PRISCILLA AHLGREN
Journal education reporter

Shauna Pettis, a sixth grader at Lancaster Elementary School, didn't always admit to her mother that she had homework.

"I wanted to go outside and play, and she wouldn't let me if she knew I had homework," explained Shauna, 11.

But Shauna and her classmates at Lancaster, 4931 N. 68th St., probably won't be able to con their parents into as much extra playtime this year. Thanks to a new homework hot line, parents now can take matters into their own hands and dial up the children's assignments.

"Hi, this is Miss Rouiller. Thank you for calling our homework hot line," starts the recorded message from sixth grade teacher Carol Rouiller. "Working together will help your child reach his greatest potential.

"Today's assignments are: 'Window by the Sea' workbook — pages 21 and 22; social studies — vocabulary, page 10 (you must have the definitions) and questions on page 13; math — page 14, [questions] 1 through 8, page 15, [questions] 4 through 12, and practice sheet 7. That's all we have today."

Please see **Homework** *page 7*

The homework hot-line

Lisa and I outside the studio where we filmed for American Express

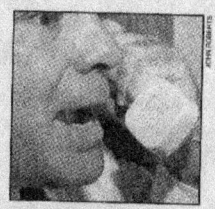

Me on the cover of The Business Journal

Our article in The Business Journal

Governor Thompson and I

The Evolution of Illusion

Love Birds

Peggy and Mom in Naples

Me, Peggy, Tiffani, and Teres
1998

Candace, Emily, Me, Cynthia, Tiffani, and Teres
1998

My family, all the grandkids included! There's Alexandria, Jonah, Gabrielle, and Andre

1998

The boat fire

John passing a barge on his right

John and I in Naples

Entering New York. Me above, and John below

Arriving in New York

Me with the Statue of Liberty in the background

The World Trade Center

June 29, 2004

My Grandfather in the middle, Dominic to his right
The Romano family estimated 1915-1920
Aunts and Uncles I never met

The Author's Note

This book has been written out of necessity. I wrote this book not only for my own benefit, but for the benefit of others that may have struggled in similar situations. The pain and anguish I have suffered all my life has been unbearable. It's a hidden pain. If you were to visit someone at a hospital today, and see their physical wounds, you would know they were hurting. But you can't see the pain of people like me. Those who've been given up, not knowing who their true parents are. The pain doesn't show like a broken bone does. There are millions of people in the world who seek to know the truth; the truth about their origin, their parents, and their culture. My message to all those fathers and mothers who have given up a child should step up and let them know. No child should have to grow up wondering who their real parents are. The few that find out later in life still will not heal. All those years of anguish have cut deep wounds, and things can never be made up. It's too late once relatives have died, and you've missed your last chance. My heart goes out to all those orphans, adopted children, and those like me. My message to all of you: be strong. And for my family: "I'll see you in my dreams." (Cliff Edwards)

~Proudly, Vincent W Romano

P.S. *Edited by Madelynne Katsma*

www.ingramcontent.com/pod-product-compliance
Lightning Source LLC
Chambersburg PA
CBHW071614080526
44588CB00010B/1132